Working with Universities

How businesses and universities can work together profitably

Adam Jolly

crimson

Working with Universities

This third edition published in Great Britain 2014 by Crimson Publishing Ltd,
19–21c Charles Street, Bath BA1 1HX

Author: Adam Jolly

British Library Cataloguing in Publication Data
A catalogue record for this book is available from the British Library.

ISBN 978 1 78059 136 0

Typeset by IDSUK (DataConnection) Ltd
Printed and bound in Malta by Gutenberg Press Ltd

Contents

Contents

Contents

Foreword

The UK's world-leading universities play an ever more central role in building future economic value, whether in specific businesses or in the economy as a whole. Universities are not only trainers of the next generation of talent, but pioneers on the front lines of research – developing the knowledge which can be translated into business reality in the form of innovative processes, products and services. And there are huge opportunities, as society seeks answers to major challenges and whole new markets open up as a result.

To reflect this, universities increasingly have a third priority alongside their research and education mandates: enterprise. Enterprise, working in and with business, is increasingly a core part of what they do.

This enterprise focus has many aspects, including nurturing the growing numbers of graduates who are creating their own businesses, and finding commercial applications for research through licences and spin-outs.

At Innovate UK we are particularly well placed to observe another, perhaps even more important aspect – universities becoming an integral part of the wider innovation system, working with businesses, whether large or small, at each stage of their innovation journeys.

As the UK's innovation agency we have encouraged these collaborations from our beginnings in 2007, when we took on board and began to build on a portfolio of innovative research and development projects which often brought together businesses and universities. And, in fact, some of our programmes have a much longer history at the university/business interface, such as the successful Knowledge Transfer Partnerships scheme, which celebrates its 40th birthday in 2015. Others, such as Innovation Vouchers, are a relatively new part of our offering.

As you would expect from the growth of university enterprise offices and technology transfer departments, we are usually pushing at an open door. Universities want to work with business, and they want to get involved in developments which will demonstrate the real world impact and economic value of what they do.

So what does this mean for business? As an entrepreneur, whether in a large or small company, you can test your ideas, ask for expert perspectives and bring in academic talent; you can buy in a technique, advance a product or join a knowledge network. Universities now offer a variety of options which are worth exploring as a route to growth by any business.

So I am pleased to welcome the publication of a new edition of this book, which contains a wealth of information on how best to work with universities for mutual advantage and for the future growth of this country.

More information can be found at www.gov.uk/government/organisations/innovate-uk

Dr Debbie Buckley-Golder,
Head of Research Engagement,
Innovate UK

SMART MONEY
FOR BRIGHT BUSINESSES

Our £5.24 million scheme is now open to SMEs and start-ups within or serving the medical technology, assisted living and telehealth sectors.

See if you qualify for a package of free support and even a cash grant to take your business idea further, faster.

Just call us on:
0845 196 4205

Find out more at:
medtechcampus.com

Anglia Ruskin
MedTech Campus
Chelmsford Harlow Southend-on-Sea

Delivered across the **East of England** by:

Acknowledgements

This book draws on the experience, expertise, inspiration and commitment of many of those who have put so much into realising the potential for collaboration between those at the forefront of knowledge and those who know how to take ideas to market.

I am particularly grateful to everyone at the Technology Strategy Board, the Intellectual Property Office, PraxisUnico, Interface, Universities UK, University Alliance, AURIL (Association for University Research and Industry Links) the Higher Education Funding Council for England, Research Councils UK, the European Patent Office and the Organisation for Economic Co-operation and Development for their generosity and patience in giving me their input and guidance. In combination, it is a powerful machine that is being created to help turn knowledge and talent into commercial reality.

I was also fortunate to speak to many of the most active and influential participants in the innovative space that lies between universities and the market. I would like to thank all those in knowledge transfer offices, business incubators, enterprise centres, careers offices, funding agencies and innovation labs who were happy to straighten out my thinking and point me in the right direction.

On the other side of the equation, I have drawn wherever possible on the insights of entrepreneurs and executives based on their experience of running projects with universities. As always, it is easy to overlook the risks and the challenges that such innovators run in taking ideas to market. My hope is that their business sense is reflected in how this book has been structured and written.

Finally, I am grateful to everyone at Crimson Publishing for their faith and their commitment in this project. The story of how universities fit into the challenge of growing a business has been a fascinating one to tell. It is a plot that is set to continue unfolding dynamically, I am sure, so I would be interested in any comments you have on what has happened so far and what might happen next.

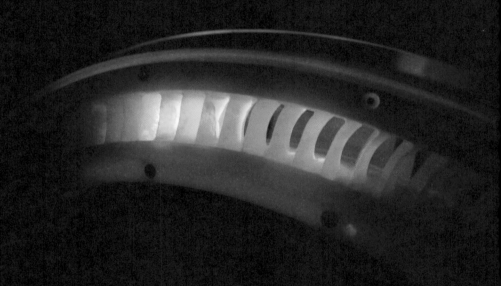

PART 1
Growth potential

BIRMINGHAM CITY
University

Services for all businesses

With innovative training, talented graduates, award-winning knowledge transfer and a strong track record of challenging business thinking, we are well placed to help your company or organisation to succeed.

An industry-inspired university, accredited by over 40 professional bodies with recognised specialist expertise used by some of the world's leading organisations, Birmingham City University is committed to working with businesses that are central to the backbone of our teaching, research and consultancy.

We can support you through:

- Consultancy and partnerships
- Training and development
- Specialist research and expertise
- Recruiting our talented graduates.

To find out more, please visit our website at **www.bcu.ac.uk/business**, send an email to **business@bcu.ac.uk** specifying the support you require or call us on **0121 331 5252**.

 BCU for Business

@BCU4Biz

1

The value of universities to entrepreneurs

Looking to get an idea off the ground? Universities can open up a package of expertise, talent, funding, networks and space for you

How can I best cut my energy bill and work out how much tax I am going to pay on my carbon? These were questions that Paul Cannon's customers kept asking him. He never really felt he or his competitors were giving a good enough answer.

Yes, he could dig out the raw data for them, but how about a clear set of signals in real time on the factory floor or on a commercial site? Three years ago, Cannon began a search for this type of solution through two local universities.

After building up a business as an electrical contractor in Leeds, he handed over day-to-day control to his son, Christopher, and now spends five days a week pursuing innovation with a team of eight in a hub for enterprise on the campus at the University of Bradford.

So far, through a combination of academic expertise and student talent, he reckons that he can cut anyone's energy bill by at least 10% and maybe even 25%. Along the way, he has also discovered a ground-breaking use of harmonics for spotting any leaks, whether of gas in the factory or oil on the seabed.

"If we had just left these questions to ourselves at Cannon Electrical, we would be nowhere near where we are now," says Cannon. "We have only reached this point with the help of academics and students."

His starting point in finding a more satisfactory response to his customers was to source a smart meter from Nanjing Bluestar in China. Its output was adequate for a professional electrician but too technical for anyone else.

Through the Yorkshire Innovation Fund, he won £3,000 for Sheffield Hallam University to build an easy-to-read spreadsheet in Excel that could be accessed remotely through the web. "Anyone can now see what electricity they are using, what it is costing and how many units of carbon are burning," says Cannon, who has now become the UK's sole importer for Nanjing Bluestar.

But what about a handheld signal to warn you when you are about to start incurring extra costs or penalties? Through a £5,000 grant at the University of Bradford, Cannon started to explore a more graphic set of signals to spark anyone into action.

For the sake of simplicity, he was looking to move his data from a server to the cloud and adopt the Raspberry Pi, a microcomputer costing £27 for use in education. To Cannon's mind, it was ideal for his customers on site, because it is as small as a pack of cards and you can just buy another one if you drop it or lose it.

For Cannon, it had other advantages. Because it is open source, he can call on a local network of programmers to refine his software, as well as bringing in students to work on different applications. He is confident that the results of all these different contributions are as good as those of any other smart meter. His challenge now is to raise the funds to invest in marketing, or find an industrial partner.

In the meantime, he has found another source of waste that his customers are finding difficult or expensive to control: leaks. "The hissing you hear in most factories is the sound of compressed air expensively escaping," he says. "Leaks are hard to find, so everyone just accepts the background noise."

Might the use of sensitive microphones give a better idea of what was happening though? Through a £10,000 grant from the TSB, the University of Bradford last year pursued a rigorous scientific inquiry for him.

It confirmed that Cannon's instincts were right: harmonic vibrations can alert you to leaks, as well as giving you a lot more information about the speed of any flow in the pipe and the performance of any machinery, such as valves.

For Cannon, it opens up the possibility of creating a clip to put on a pipe at a much lower cost than his customers currently pay to insert a monitor. He is also starting to think he might be able to replace deep-sea divers who have to check for any leaks of oil and gas from pipelines on the sea bed.

For other entrepreneurs and innovators, universities can be equally valuable partners not just in creating breakthroughs and innovations, but in making improvements and finding fixes. Through the university, you can gain access to the combination of knowledge, talent, funding, networks and space that you need to grow.

Access to knowledge

Academic researchers are on the frontline of knowledge. They are asking the questions and making the discoveries that are going to create future value within the economy.

The time lines on which they are working may well be too extended for you. But academics also have the expertise within their field to lay out all the options and point you in the right direction to sort out your challenges in real time.

Even in a medium-sized research university, you will find a thousand academics working on nearly all aspects of human endeavour. Science. Commerce. Design. Digital media. Put the right question to the right academic and you will get a rigorous answer that can lift your whole business. You might be surprised by the enthusiasm of the response from experts who are going to see their technology appear in the real world for the first time.

The chances of having such a meaningful dialogue are improving all the time. Over the last 10 years, universities have put in place mechanisms to handle projects of all sizes. Like Cannon Electrical, you can start with short, initial studies and build up into more ambitious collaborations.

Access to talent

In attracting the best minds to answer the toughest questions, universities act as another source of competitive advantage for smaller companies: training graduates in the high-level scientific, commercial and creative skills on which future economic performance is going to depend.

As they have in transferring knowledge, universities are developing a more flexible set of mechanisms for smaller enterprises to access that talent. Alongside traditional recruitment, you can bring in graduates on internships and placements at any point in the year, not just at the end of the summer term.

Access to funding

This flow of knowledge and talent into the economy is becoming central to public policy. Universities are becoming leading players in supporting business regionally and nationally. They are often able to draw on public funds to make different forms of collaboration happen.

Many, for instance, run innovation vouchers worth between £3,000 and £5,000 to encourage initial projects between universities and SMEs. All are heavily engaged in placing graduates within business to pursue innovative projects, saving you two-thirds of the normal cost. Most can advise you on how to set up collaboration in such a way to draw on national or European schemes. Some enterprises are even participating in funded consortiums as a way of driving their growth.

As well as public funds, the commercial teams at universities, particularly those in enterprise and innovation centres, have good links with local networks of investors or may even be running their own funds. Alongside such equity, more and more are looking to turn it into "smart money" by bringing in coaches and advisers to keep your plan on track.

Platforms for growth

Such proximity to those in the know can make all the difference in launching an innovation. It is no coincidence that Cannon Electrical's spin-out, Intenwatch, is now located on campus at Bradford. It has put them in a good position to keep bouncing ideas off the research team, staying in touch with the university's commercial office and recruiting students.

Many universities now offer space to ventures under their wing with a view to letting them grow flexibly. Usually, these are accompanied by a business advisory service. You can start as a virtual tenant, before taking a desk or a room in an incubator. Once you scale up, you can then move to offices at the innovation centre and even run operations on a business park.

Whether or not you are located on campus, you can keep yourself in the flow of ideas, look for solutions and spot potential candidates by joining any one of a number of business-to-academic networks. Your local university will be able to plug you into anything relevant. At the national level, a series of specialist networks are run through the Technology Strategy Board, which you are free to join.

As well as their traditional role in mapping out the future, universities are becoming an integral part of what anyone in business can achieve today. So would Paul Cannon recommend forming a relationship with a university like Bradford? "Without a doubt," he says. "It is giving us a new lease of life."

2

How universities are changing

Universities are findings new ways to develop technology for the market

Universities no longer operate as isolated centres of pure research, but are becoming an integral part of the overall innovation system. More than ever, new growth in the economy largely depends on the primary knowledge and expertise they generate.

Many of these intellectual assets have always leaked into the market through published papers and recent graduates, but their value has rarely been fully captured. Hepcetin, the Herceptin treatment for breast cancer, is just one recent example. The underlying science was brilliantly invented in Britain in the 90s, but it was profitably commercialised as a product in the US. Beyond the prestige, we have less to show for our originality than we might.

In the last 20 years, a systematic effort has been made to add a commercial dimension to the core activities of universities in research and teaching. For academics, it amounts to a fundamental change in their culture. They can no longer just invent and publish, as in the case of Herceptin, but have to take into account the impact they are making in business and on society.

In the latest evaluation of funding for research in the UK, this commitment has been formally enshrined for the first time: 20% of any award now depends on impact. At the same time, targets for engaging with industry are starting to be written into the contracts of many researchers.

Yet universities remain a long way from the market. The journey from an early-stage finding in the lab to a fully realised product is one of the most complex, unpredictable and expensive tasks in business. However good the underlying science, any number of commercial risks can derail its transformation.

To manage the process of engagement, universities have developed a professional capability for transferring their knowledge. In the place of the single officer for industrial liaison that many had in the 1990s, you will find teams of up to 70, who specialise in areas such as research partnerships, contract negotiations, consultancy, licensing and spin-outs.

However, the original hopes that this transactional model might result in significant streams of income have been largely misplaced, particularly for smaller universities. For every hit, most have experienced many more misses.

No-one can wait on the value to emerge from intellectual property alone. Softer forms of engagement such as the transfer of know-how and expertise often lead to faster, more reliable returns.

Similarly, academics rarely turn into entrepreneurs and few spin-outs move beyond the innovation centre. Ventures with the capacity to employ thousands, as we know from experience in the US, tend to come from elsewhere within the wider university and its networks.

So a broader, more reciprocal definition is being given to how universities can best work with business. Knowledge exchange, instead of technology transfer, is evolving as the term to describe the two-way flow between those in the lab and those in the market.

As highly complex institutions, the challenge for universities is how best to create a commercial culture without undermining the fundamental integrity of the research apparatus. Conflicts inevitably occur between the public and the private; and between the commercial and the scientific.

At the University of Manchester, which has just re-written its IP policy, the response has been a bold one: "We are opening up the campus and all our corridors to business," says Tony Walker, director of research and business development at Manchester's commercial arm, UMIP. "We want to let them be part of the conversation to stimulate new opportunity."

His team looks after 5,000 academics who between them disclose about 400 inventions a year. "Our capacity to absorb projects is limited," he says. "So we are looking to shift the curve and reach out externally."

His goal is to explore new ways of building relationships with business to improve the chances of technologies and insights making an impact. Industry spanners, risk sharing, crowd wisdom, unipreneurs and social enterprise are just some of the techniques which he is developing.

Industry spanners

Across the university, Walker is inviting in entrepreneurs to talk to researchers who are at the early stages of developing an idea. His hope is that they will improve the university's discernment around the technologies it starts to develop when a potential user says at the early stages of a proposal: "Looks good, but have you thought about this? How about something else? Or tried an adjacent strategy? Maybe even do not even bother."

In the physics department, for instance, eight entrepreneurs with a feel for the culture within a university were pre-matched to nine academic ideas with the potential for industrial application, which has led to three specific projects. "As a result, we have improved our insight and validation," says Walker. "Projects are moving forward more quickly and we can seed other ideas."

Risk sharing

Traditionally, the university would look to push its technology into the market through licences to SME users. Now, it is considering more entrepreneurial solutions. In joint collaborations, academics work directly alongside the entrepreneur and may even join the company in exchange for equity.

Similarly, in working with industrial partners, the university will consider co-funding the challenges that its academics are asked to pursue. For instance, an innovation centre in Cumbria is being developed with leading energy suppliers and public agencies to develop new solutions and revive capabilities in the supply chain for nuclear technology.

Crowd wisdom

Further insights from industry are gathered by releasing showcases for future research onto social networks and innovation platforms. Potential users of any resulting technology can vote on what are likely to be its most useful applications.

Anyone who is interested in pursuing the results further can then sign up and start working on the inside. "For the university, it means we have industry in mind from the start," says Walker.

Unipreneurs

Student entrepreneurs are encouraged throughout the university. For those who have ideas with potential as technology applications, Walker runs a programme to test the validity of their ideas, bring in mentors, line up the intellectual property and screen potential sources of funding.

Similarly, all those taking a doctorate are given training in enterprise and encouraged to think about the commercial applications for their ideas as they write up their thesis. A panel of entrepreneurs then screens their ideas and awards funding to prove a concept.

Creating entrepreneurs

To support the growing numbers of student entrepreneurs, the University of Leeds like many others is now running its own start-up service, SPARK. It is designed as the first port of call for anyone from any department who wants to test and develop their ideas.

"One day I might be speaking to a student with the seed of an idea and the next discussing a full business plan," says Kairen Skelley, the head of SPARK. "We can help at every stage. Many students don't have the practical business knowledge – or enough of it – to really drive their idea forward. Through our workshops and one-to-one sessions we can work with a student or graduate to really develop the idea and the business plan, so they can start their business with confidence."

One business Skelley has supported is Wireless Medical, which is the result of four medical students spotting an unmet need in the NHS. They won £2,000 in a business plan competition for their wireless heart monitor and were then awarded an enterprise scholarship. Funded by the university's alumni, these scholarships are designed to give student entrepreneurs practical and financial support, as well as sending them on a boot camp to develop their plans. As a result, Wireless Medical is close to developing a prototype and is looking for a partner to carry out clinical trials.

Alongside SPARK, the Leeds Enterprise Centre is a focal point for enterprise education on campus. Its modules are wide ranging, starting at the foundations for enterprise, innovation and leadership, then covering more practical issues such as finance and social networking. All count as credits within a student's degree.

The two-week module for second year medical students that the founders of Wireless Medical elected to take is an example of how enterprises can start in unexpected places, says Dr Sarah Underwood at the Leeds Enterprise Centre. "It gave them the chance to develop their enterprise skills and apply them to a genuine issue."

Social enterprise

In reaching out as widely as possible to academics, Walker accepts that for many the financial incentives for engaging with business are relatively weak. Their research and teaching will always come first.

Only 8% regularly disclose their ideas. However, all are interested in the proliferation of their work, particularly as their careers might now depend on it. Social enterprise can often be a more attractive option for them.

One recent example came from the department of architecture. A researcher identified a way of restoring the lighting in 40,000 Turkish baths across North Africa. Although an important part of the social fabric, they are close to falling into dilapidation because of the rising cost of power.

A partnership is now being formed with a social entrepreneur to bring in the supply chain around Manchester. "Our solution is a blend of ancient history, social science and solar technology," says Walker. "It has never been on anyone's radar."

These are the kinds of opportunity that only a university can create, says Walker. "The value is out there, if we can build the right kinds of relationship to make it happen."

Expert comment by Alice Frost, Higher Education Funding Council for England

What is knowledge exchange?

Many university subjects – from engineering, science, social science and business through to art and design – have relevance to business. Knowledge and expertise in universities can help with product and process innovations in businesses, as well as organisational design, branding and marketing, and professional development for enterprise and innovation.

Universities have long recognised that knowledge and research developed through higher education (HE) have value for businesses and economic growth as well as for wider society, such as for health or culture. This started originally with technology transfer licensing university intellectual property (IP) to business or creating new IP-based companies (often called "spin-outs"). However, the range of research, knowledge and expertise in universities has wider economic relevance and application beyond technology transfer – the many different forms of unlocking this value are now all referred to as knowledge exchange (KE). They include:

- **collaborative and contract research**
- **consultancy**
- **access to specialist equipment in universities and colleges**
- **IP**
- **development of professional capabilities to use knowledge (CPD).**

Focus on SMEs

While all businesses may benefit from university knowledge exchange, SMEs may find it particularly difficult to access this as they may have less capacity and time to link with universities compared to big companies. HEFCE recognises this in the way it funds universities which work with SMEs through Higher Education Innovative Funding (HEIF). HEIF is allocated to universities on the basis of a formula related to income from users for all forms of KE activity (businesses, public and third sectors). HEFCE double-weights income from SMEs in the HEIF formula, so the higher costs for universities who work with SMEs are recognised. This helps universities to have professional capabilities in place to understand and respond to the particular problems of SMEs. Universities have a culture of openness, and often help SMEs particularly with business-focused networking, connecting them with other SMEs and with larger businesses, experts, funders, etc.

Alice Frost, head of business and community policy, Higher Education Funding Council for England

3

Change the game

Future growth is happening now within universities

In late 2013, a venture that converts data into text floated on AIM. Capitalised at £100m, its value soared on its first days on the market to £290m. Four years earlier, it was still a research project in natural language generation (NLG) at the University of Aberdeen.

By questioning the boundaries of conventional knowledge, academics, such those at Aberdeen, are prone to making radical discoveries that can turn expectations upside down and re-define the rules by which markets work. Even if few spin-outs make it all the way to AIM, universities, according to recent remarks by the OECD, are the primary source of the intellectual assets that are expected to drive future, sustainable growth in the economy.

In Aberdeen, the original inspiration for December's flotation lay in the collaboration between two colleagues in the department of computing science and an expert in weather forecasts. Together they were investigating the potential for condensing data from multiple sources into messages on which someone could make a decision. It led them into the relatively uncharted territory of NLG.

Soon they found themselves fielding queries from numerous other industries, notably oil and gas. It put them in the unusual position of being forced to consider a spin-out. Branded as Data2Text, they moved to a special corridor for university ventures. From the start, they were trading profitably and had no need to raise external capital.

Essentially, they were putting themselves in an unexpectedly strong competitive position by combining solutions to two technical challenges: first, they developed the analytics to capture expert knowledge from large sets of data and, then, they generated messages as a narrative, rather than as numbers or graphics. For international business, it opened up the prospect of releasing the value in all their "big data" by making any analysis easy to follow for any given audience.

As the extent of the market for big data started to reveal itself, Data2Text collaborated with a commercial software house, Arria, who bought 20% of their shares in 2012 and kept an option to buy the rest. Originally, the assumption was that NLG could be integrated into existing processes. In fact, it soon became clear that it represented a global opportunity in itself with applications in any business collecting large amounts of data from multiple sources, such as health and finance.

Last year, Arria bought up the remaining shares and raised £25m in new capital from private investors. It then floated on AIM with a view to raising its profile, as well as creating enough liquidity in its shares to attract future talent and equity.

The university, as well as the founders, have each retained an approximately 5% stake in the floated business. Since December, the shares have fallen back to a more realistic level, but all of them are still sitting on a profit worth several million on paper.

For the university, the other benefit is that Arria has chosen it as a base for a research centre into how NLG might now develop. Both academics have chosen to remain on campus.

Radical science rarely translates into a platform technology at the same speed and scale as Data2Text. However, like other universities, Aberdeen has developed a comprehensive set of processes to identify any research with commercial potential. Each year, its academics make 30–40 disclosures, of which perhaps two turn into spin-outs.

The commercial team stays in close touch with potential investors. In late 2013 and early 2014, the market for flotations looked to be opening up again, says Dr Elizabeth Rattray, deputy director of research and innovation at Aberdeen. "It is a good sign for investors to come back and invest in early-stage ideas."

The cycle for venture capital also varies, she says. "Sometimes platform technologies are all the rage, when you can set the potential against high requirements for cash. More usually, the emphasis is on finding a niche with a clear route to market."

Aberdeen also supports spin-outs directly as a way of encouraging others to co-invest, In life sciences, which typically take longer to reach market than digital media, it is contributing to a £47m fund in partnership with the universities of Glasgow and Edinburgh, as well as Scottish Enterprise and Eli Lilley.

Following the flotation of Arria, Aberdeen's next priority is to capitalise on its strengths in digital enterprise by setting up an incubator with the city council and Robert Gordon University. Inspired by the example of Data2Text, the aim is to support students and staff who have ideas for developing technologies that could fuel a new wave of spin-outs and start-ups in north-east Scotland and beyond.

Innovation models

Bridge building? Open sourcing? Pre-competitive IP? Technology ready? Innovation is picking up speed in universities

Alzheimer's represents one of the most urgent challenges we all face. By 2050, nearly a third of us in the developed world will be over 65, the age at which cognitive decline escalates rapidly. Without any treatment, the costs to us as individuals and as citizens could become overwhelming.

Even though we have known for 30 years about the protein that is most likely to cause the decay of our neurons, we are as far as ever from an answer. Countless studies have been undertaken and 10 major clinical studies, each costing $200m–$300m, have failed. Some estimate that the total cost of all these wasted efforts could be as high as £20bn and argue that finding a solution could be as tough as putting a man on Mars.

One response being developed at the University of Oxford is taking a radical approach to the innovation process itself. Too many studies are pursued in secret, it is argued, leading to too much duplication and waste. Instead, it would pay if innovators could adopt a more open, collaborative approach in researching basic science before they ever reach the point at which they might start to compete.

Initial support for exploring this new path came from the Wellcome Trust and eight pharma companies are now paying £5m over four years to take part in the Structural Genomics Consortium, which is seeking to identify new targets for a range of conditions, including cancer and neuro-psychiatry, as well as Alzheimer's.

All its findings are being openly released for scrutiny by the wider academic community. Most will fail. Once any potential winners are clinically validated, the pharma companies can start to develop their own molecules which they are free to protect.

When they are spending £20m to test a single novel target for clinical use, their investment represents good value, says the consortium's chief scientist, Professor Chas Bountra. For him, the benefits of working pre-competitively are that expertise is pooled, resources are combined and risks are shared. "You can then gain access to the best scientists and clinicians, as well as working closely with regulators and patients."

Bridge building

As with the Alzheimer's challenge, other innovations in business and society are less and less likely to be found by drawing on a single source of inspiration and then pushing it through into commercial use. Such a linear model is becoming too expensive and slow.

You can no longer just wait on answers to emerge, when competition is so intense and expectations from users so high. It makes more sense to cross boundaries and look outside for ideas. In a world of instant communication, you have the chance to draw on the brightest and best, wherever they are.

In pursuit of innovation, many bridges are now being built between all those with an interest in resolving a particular challenge. Often gathered round a university, actors such as scientists, public agencies, users, charities and investors are coming together with the goal of co-creating ideas and growth.

Such open innovation is defined as the "close collaboration by all stakeholders in addressing a business or social challenge" by Professor Birgitte Andersen at the Big Innovation Centre. Resources such as knowledge, finance, people, markets, big data and intellectual property are typically pooled.

"But it is more than simply sharing risk and reward," she says. "It encapsulates the integration of the entire innovation ecosystem."

Open sourcing

The principle of opening up a business to ideas from unexpected sources and from disciplines outside its normal range is being pursued by a brand like L'Oreal. It has developed a tool to check out the whole world of research and IP whenever a question is raised and to identify potential solutions wherever they are. The system is deliberately designed to bring in ideas from off-field, not just recognised centres of expertise.

Equally, L'Oreal runs partnerships with 200 universities in the belief that it can never stop looking for innovation, but that it is becoming almost impossible to manage it all in-house. Its aim is to import ideas from many different fields and access knowledge from all parts of a university.

In parallel with these relationships with the knowledge base, it is seeking to democratise innovation through crowd-sourcing and give millions of users the chance to contribute to the development of future products.

Competitions

Another way of fast-tracking ideas is through competitions, which are now being widely adopted by major businesses and by public agencies. A pharma company like Bayer, for instance, has awarded a hundred grants of between £4,000 and £100,000 over the last four years for researchers to investigate potential targets for new drugs. It treats the knowledge as pre-competitive, so the intellectual property remains with the applicant, who is free to publish the results. Bayer will only consider filing a patent once it develops its own molecule.

The Technology Strategy Board (TSB) also favours the use of competitions to remove roadblocks to the growth of a high-value idea. Often working in combination with universities or other partners, it posts an average of one competition a week. In value, they vary from £20,000 for feasibility studies to multi-million pound programmes. A short, sharp challenge over six months is a format that the TSB often favours.

Cross-disciplinary challenges

In innovation, many of the best ideas tend to come when one discipline crosses into another. It is at these interfaces that the most unexpected and productive connections can happen.

Many of the major challenges in public policy, such as the ageing population, zero carbon, intelligent transport or future cities, now depend on combining research from numerous sources and pulling together teams of different experts.

A simple division into traditional academic disciplines is no longer enough at most universities. Instead, they are adopting a matrix structure and creating a series of cross-disciplinary research centres, which are open to many different sources of innovation and which can work with all those with a stake in finding a solution.

Strategic relationships

To stay ahead of the game, many businesses are now building strategic relationships with universities. Instead of importing results from research, as they once did, they are looking to generate a free flow of ideas and talent. Typically, they move onto the campus and fund a centre to pursue fundamental ideas that could re-define their industry.

Rolls-Royce has eight such long-term relationships with universities around the world, for instance. By working with an engineering department like the one at Sheffield, it puts itself in a better position to attract the best talent and follow the latest thinking than if it remained on its own site in Derby.

To inspire a free flow of ideas, such relationships are governed by trust, based on a set of rules for the fair ownership and use of any intellectual property that is generated. The goal is to create a platform on which everyone is encouraged to bring forward innovations.

Mobility

The principle of mobility is one that many universities now pursue. They are setting up long internships for their master's students. They are bringing in industrial engineers to their labs. They are putting their professors on the boards of companies. They are encouraging executives to swap roles with academics for 10 days.

All these switches can speed up the transfer of knowledge. One producer of scientific instruments, who placed a programmer with the University of Bristol, reckons the process of developing a new piece of code became five times quicker.

Technology ready

Numerous risks remain in taking an idea from concept into use. Britain has a strong record in creating new knowledge (phases 1 to 3 of the TSB's measure for technology readiness) and in building a market (phases 7 to 9), but is weaker in phases 4 to 6 (giving demonstrations, producing prototypes and running pilots).

A series of initiatives is being pursued to bridge this gap. Through the TSB, seven catapults have recently been set up to cut the risks of developing technologies in high-growth markets that could take off globally.

Designed as halfway houses between scientific inquiry and commercial development, the catapults will help start-ups commercialise their ideas and they will run collaborations with major players to drive improvements through the supply chain.

For anyone developing a product, exclusivity will be retained. But in making process improvements, innovation will usually be pursued as an open collaboration in which the intellectual property is freely shared. Significant gains in productivity, for instance, are already being made in this way through the High-value manufacturing centre.

Whether tightening up the supply chain or searching for a cure to Alzheimer's, shared innovation is challenging old models for how researchers and companies can best work together.

The seven catapults

1. High Value Manufacturing
2. Cell Therapy
3. Offshore Renewable Energy
4. Satellite Applications
5. Connected Digital Economy
6. Future Cities
7. Transport Systems

Further details: www.catapult.org.uk

5

Growth hubs

Universities are creating platforms for enterprises to explore how they can grow their ideas

Last December, the Engine Shed re-opened its doors to Bristol's next generation of entrepreneurs and innovators. Part of Brunel's original design for the station at Temple Meads, it is now a platform for those looking to accelerate ideas in the city.

In a joint £2m project, the university and the city council have combined to create a hub targeted at innovations with the potential for high growth. Only 20% of those who occupy the 40,000 sq ft are expected to come directly from the university. The rest will be ambitious local ventures.

Some might be proto-entrepreneurs. Others might already have 20 employees. All will feel the benefit of working alongside the university to line up expertise and resources. Equally, the university will have a ready pool of potential collaborators on which to call when it puts in its own bids for research funding.

For the Engine Shed, the emphasis is deliberately on testing out potential winners fast. Unlike a managed office, rent starts low in the early stages then escalates as the business grows.

The re:centre: Bradford's £6m portal for enterprise to access the university

A team of advisers, including an entrepreneur in residence, actively seeks to resolve any technical, legal or financial challenges by making introductions and opening up networks. Often, 10 minutes over coffee with the right academic can save days of wasted effort.

It is a formula that is already proving effective. Over the last eight years, the University of Bristol has run its business incubator in tandem with four other universities in the south (Bath, Southampton, Surrey and Exeter). Collectively known as Set Squared, they were recently rated as fourth best in the world and the first in Europe.

At the Engine Shed, the target is to continue raising £20m–£30m a year for the 50–60 companies which are in residence at any one time. But it is also taking on a wider role as part of the enterprise zone that Bristol's LEP (local economic partnership) is creating to focus support for smaller companies.

An independent accelerator for web ventures is already operating from the Engine Shed. After an initial round of funding through the crowd, participants are given a 13-week chance to make a business case, before a decision is taken on whether they will make it through to the next phase.

Two broader initiatives are designed to widen the Engine Shed's reach. Anyone checking out an idea can rent a 'high-performance desk', which gives them work space in Bristol, as well as Bath and London. Then, all those currently using the Engine Shed are given the chance to draw on the energy and know-how of previous occupants and corporate executives in a regular business lounge.

Although the Engine Shed is still in its early stage of development, the LEP may well start to ask whether its combination of activities, service and networks might amount to a new model for smaller companies to engage with the universities around Bristol. Instead of picking off projects one by one, might it be easier to build a wider set of relationships through a hub, such as the Engine Shed?

For universities like Bristol, this kind of engagement with entrepreneurs is becoming an integral part of its overall mission. As the vice-chancellor of the university, Professor Eric Thomas, has said: "A single university is not just the sum of education, research and enterprise as three separate activities. They are all inextricably integrated; each activity is inseparable from the other."

This mission to learn, teach, explore, challenge, create and grow is one that is being given new impetus at the University of Bradford through its re:centre, which opened last October.

Built with the backing of the European Regional Development Fund and HEFCE at a cost of close to £6m, the re:centre is designed as "a superhighway into the university for local enterprises to work with academics and students," says its manager for business partnerships, Michelle Miller. "We are a living lab with the goal of being as accessible as we can."

Built of timber and hemp, the building is one of the most environmentally ambitious in Europe. Inside, it is designed as an open space to bring in ideas and set up collaborations.

Tenants can use it in two main ways. For those pursuing their own ideas, they can use the shared space on the first floor for £10 a week. Or a business can take a unit on the top floor with room for eight people for £100 a week, which is close to the going rate in Bradford, but has the advantage of opening up all the facilities in the university.

Everyone has the chance to draw on business support, academic advice and student talent. Once an idea starts to grow, the assumption is that a business can move on and the creative process can start with someone else all over again.

"For the university, it opens up our scope and we want to break the barriers as much as possible," says Miller. "We are looking to bring in people who would never have thought of working with us before and make it as easy as possible for them."

6

Research leverage

Use grants to prove your technology and build an efficient capital structure

By working through universities such as Glasgow, Strathclyde, Exeter, Plymouth and Southampton, Witt Energy is putting itself in a position to create a platform technology. Since starting up four years ago, it has grown through sourcing a series of grants to prove each stage of its technology, then raised a small amount of equity to develop the results, before starting the process again.

According to Bill Corr at Scottish Enterprise who helped set up Witt's first feasibility study with Glasgow, it has become the best leveraged venture he has ever seen. "They have used everything out there to minimise the risk to themselves and their investors," he says. "As well as leveraging funds from the Technology Strategy Board, they have made use of R&D tax credits and ensured that any investments qualify for relief.

"If they had put together a five-year technology plan, they might be a year ahead of where they are now, but it would have involved a much higher level of risk. Instead, they are always looking at what it will take to reach the next level. They always look at their current requirement for funding, then bring in investors, which was often for less than £100,000 early on."

By raising less than a million pounds in total, the founders still control most of the equity in the business. "Once they launch their first product in the autumn, they will have lots of scope for when they do want to raise finance big time," says Corr, who has helped numerous innovative ventures to raise funds.

Witt's potential for growth is based on an elegantly simple idea which no-one thought possible. The exception was Martin Wickett, a civil engineer. He refused to accept that the chaotic motion all around us in the natural world could not be captured as a source of power whether at sea, in the wind and when we move. His solution works like a self-winding watch except that it captures all six dimensions of motion. But was it anything more than an interesting principle? Through a £5,000 voucher for innovation, the head of mechanical engineering at the University of Glasgow reviewed the technology.

"He did an amazing job in confirming that we could collect six degrees of motion and turn it into power," says Mairi Wickett, Martin's wife and now Wickett's managing director. "He gave us a comprehensive report on how a device could be built so it was maintenance free without any external blades or parts.

"For an investor worried that a technology might be too blue sky, the universities do give credibility. The only frustration," she says, "is when time runs over, particularly when you are trying to keep a venture going."

Another voucher bought Witt a further 10–15 days at the University of Strathclyde, which produced a mathematical model for setting the right power. Witt could then work out the size of its designs for 30 or 50 watts.

By now it was becoming clear that Witt could operate as a platform technology for all sorts of personal devices, including mobile phones. A patent is now in place in all leading markets for Witt to grow through licence.

But where did it make sense to start applying the technology first? Mairi Wickett started looking at markets that might be failing. Navigational devices, she found, could not use solar as a source of power in the northern hemisphere because it is too unreliable. Too many systems rely on an uninterrupted flow of data.

In developing products, she has just finished working with the universities of Plymouth and Exeter on a £250,000 Smart award from the Technology Strategy Board, and is about to start another one with the universities of Southampton and Strathclyde.

By using Witt's technology to power electronics and communications on a ship, Wickett now estimates that she can make a saving of 5% on the huge costs of fuel in crossing the Atlantic.

One unexpected bonus of all this work is that Witt found itself nominated for a global competition for the best new marine technology, Ocean Exchange. At the awards in Savannah last year, it won the first prize of $100,000, opening up other potential markets for its navigational buoys.

Over the last four years, says Wickett, universities have played an essential role in helping Witt to piece together its technology and its business. It is not a perfect system, she admits: universities often have a different mindset without any appreciation of the time pressures on innovative ventures and the forms for funding can be difficult to complete, unless you find someone who knows how the system works.

One final piece of assistance is now just falling into place for Witt. Bill Corr has agreed to step in as chairman, while continuing with his duties at Scottish Enterprise. "I found myself giving more help than I would normally, reviewing contracts and agreements," he says. "I am not being paid and I have no equity. If Witt becomes a global venture, then all well and good. I just want to act as an honest broker to set them on their way."

Durham University
Business & Innovation Services

Business Engagement

"Building Relationships

Employability & Placements
Internships
Recruitment & Careers
Schools Outreach
Student Enterprise Education
Student Projects

Collaborative Research Projects
Contract Research
Co-Funding of PhD Studentships
Consultancy & Analytical Services
Training & Continuous Education

EU Collaborative Funding
Research Council Funding
TSB Funding

Alumni Relations
Links to Other Partners & Contacts
Links to SMEs
Prizes & Sponsorship
Sponsored Chairs & Lectureships

Knowledge Exchange Programmes
Knowledge Transfer Partnerships
Knowledge Transfer Secondments

Sharing Excellence"

durham.business@durham.ac.uk

www.durham.ac.uk/bis

T: +44 (0)191 33 44650
F: +44 (0)191 33 44634

Maple Wing
Mountjoy Centre
Durham University
Durham, DH1 3LE

PART 2
The transfer market

Working with Services to Business

University of HUDDERSFIELD

Services to Business supports companies from all industry sectors, providing access to the extensive knowledge, skills and resources at the University of Huddersfield.

The benefits your company could access by working with the University of Huddersfield include:

- Access to innovation and knowledge to deliver new products
- Access to new talent for your company
- Training and development for your staff
- Access to new networks – academic and industrial
- Access to cutting edge facilities and equipment
- Opportunities for cross-supply-chain innovation
- Access to new funding opportunities

The University has a wealth of experience working with companies of all sizes and at all stages of product or service development. With a track record of establishing enterprising, mutually beneficial relationships, we work with you to understand and meet your objectives, finding the right people and expertise for your needs.

Whether you're a start-up with a brilliant idea or an established business looking for fresh perspectives, we provide first-rate research and testing facilities coupled with the commercial skills to help your business flourish.

If you have any business enquiries or would like to find out more about what we offer, please do not hesitate to contact any one of us- we'll be more than happy to help.

Tel 01484 473666
E-mail business@hud.ac.uk

Twitter @HudStB

7

Commercial capability

As a discipline, knowledge exchange is evolving fast

In the last 15 years, Britain's universities have been conducting a large scale experiment in how they engage with business. Previously, as an SME, you would have found yourself tracking down a lone industrial liaison officer, who was charged with looking after a thousand academics and a thousand researchers. No surprise that it was difficult to find your way around.

Now you will find yourself engaging with a specialised team that is developing a series of tools for putting the right academic together with the right business. The purpose is to let you interact as freely and as creatively as possible, while ensuring that the value in any ideas is captured.

Spurred by a belief that universities are becoming the cog around which the knowledge economy can turn, significant public funds have been put into building up their commercial capabilities. Each year, for instance, £150m is made available to England's hundred universities through a "higher education innovation fund" to support the development of their engagements with business and with SMEs in particular.

For universities, the initial task has been to create a clearer and more rewarding process for taking their own research into the market. Through this process of "technology transfer", a university would typically focus on:

- defining any intellectual property
- encouraging and supporting start-ups from graduates and students

- spinning out research into new ventures

- licensing knowledge to business partners who can bring it to market

- setting up collaborations to run research programmes.

This classic model of pushing the university's work into use is now developing into a broader definition based on a more collaborative working model with partners in business. As well as transferring their own IP, most universities are seeking to manage a more complex set of strategic relationships because they recognise that:

- an open flow of people and data across disciplines often leads to the best results

- the pull of demand in the market and challenges in society can be as strong a source of inspiration as the push of new technology

- and innovation is moving beyond its technical core in science and engineering, embracing softer forms of know-how, including disciplines like the social sciences and humanities.

As a result, most universities now refer to the process of commercial engagement as "knowledge exchange", rather than simply technology transfer, and typically employ 25–35 people in all aspects of taking ideas into the market, such as collaborations, contract negotiations, consultancy, licensing and spin-outs. In the case of research powerhouses, like Oxford or Imperial, the headcount is closer to 70 and specialist technology accelerators have been spun out as standalone companies.

Over the years, the profile of those who work in knowledge exchange has changed from a purely scientific background to draw on a much wider range of commercial experience as a way of ensuring that they can speak for both academics and business.

Ready for market

Academics, as specialists in the fundamental principles of what we know and how we apply it, remain a prime source of ideas and insights that can re-write the rules on which markets and industries are based. Each university is free to find its own way for transferring any intellectual property, but will typically encompass three functions: a scout, a pathfinder and a dealer.

- The scout will spend their time building up relationships with academics, identifying interesting ideas and encouraging their disclosure for eventual commercial use.

- The pathfinder will then check whether an idea will work technically and commercially by sounding out potential users in business, building up a profile of how a customer might look and what they might pay.

- A dealer, armed with proof that a concept works and that a market exists, will seek the right type of transaction for the university and the academic, through either a spin-out, a licence or some other form of collaboration.

Universities such as Manchester continue to run this process themselves. Others, such as Sheffield and Cardiff, have handed the process over to a company that specialises in building up a pipeline of IP from the university and commercialising it.

Ready to engage

Separate from the process of commercialising intellectual property, universities like Sheffield and Manchester are putting engagement teams into each faculty to build relationships and collaborations with business. These are expressly designed as an intelligent interface to respond as quickly as possible to any queries.

"We are fundamentally about research and teaching, not exploiting our IP," says Neale Daniele in the engineering department at the University of Sheffield. "We have gateways in all our faculties as an access point and to gather intelligence." For smaller companies, in particular, the advantage is that you can talk to someone who will understand the assumptions on which your business rests and will enable you to bring out the real question that you want to ask. The responses will vary by discipline. In the life sciences, it is more likely to be a matter for pure research. In engineering, you will be closer to market.

Outcomes

Nationally, such policies are having a significant effect, according to the Higher Education Statistics Agency:

- over the last five years, 1200 spin-outs have been created and 3600 patents have been granted
- universities are now earning £80m a year from their intellectual property
- and their income from contract research stands at £1.1bn and from collaborative research at £870m.

Overall, knowledge exchange in higher education is growing at 4% per year and now totals £3.4bn, which represents a 45% rise in real terms since 2003–04. On the basis of these figures, the UK is widely regarded as reaching the same level of performance as the US and, worldwide, now only lies behind Switzerland.

At a national level, the benefits for the UK in bringing research closer to the market are clear. For individual universities, the expectations that their IP could become a recurring source of extra income have largely proved misplaced. In reality, they are more likely to break even year on year.

The difficulty lies in commercialising complex ideas and technologies and the need for those taking major financial risks to secure a return. First you have to screen a hundred candidates, then invest in developing ten, only one of which might ever make it to market. From any proceeds, you have to meet the cost of funding the other nine.

However, for universities, these commercial activities are recognised as having a much wider set of indirect benefits:

- companies often follow up a university's inventions by asking for more data and by commissioning more research
- students want to attend universities that are creating solutions in the real world
- spin-outs start to create an active market for technology on the university's doorstep
- academics are better placed to find promising new lines of inquiry for their next research project.

Taking a longer view over the 10 years that it takes to investigate a complex technology, there is the scope for a major one-off return on sale or flotation. Typically, any proceeds are split three ways: a third to the university to invest back into its core activities; a third to the school or faculty where the idea originated; and a third to the academics to encourage them and their colleagues to keep finding ways of commercialising their knowledge.

Centres of excellence

The focus of knowledge exchange is sharpening, as universities accept that they can no longer just be "open for business".

It is unrealistic for academics to expect to field general enquiries, when they are busy with their commitments to research and teaching, says John Francis, who has been at the University of South Wales for the last two years. "If you are going to run a commercial service, you cannot be all things to all men."

His goal is to pick out strong capabilities within the university and find academics who are willing to work with business. A centre for the intelligent testing of power trains is a prime example. It specialises in telling racing teams and car manufacturers where their points of failure will ultimately occur. It recently ran a test over 120 days for a winner of Le Mans, giving a detailed report on how it broke down.

"Clients are hammering on the door and we have had to turn away an enquiry from an F1 team," says Francis. "My job is to give the academics the capacity to take on these engagements and build a series of mini business units within the university."

He is pursuing a similar initiative in tuneable lasers which is a speciality that the university has developed in opto-electronics. First, he is identifying potential users and inviting them to play with the technology. Only when they see its potential, will he start talking about any follow-up research or IP.

Other centres of excellence are being created around mobile apps for SMEs, training for financial services, cyber security and renewable energy amongst others. "We want to make sure we manage the expectations of any customers and complete our work on time. Otherwise we will refer it elsewhere."

8

Approaching a university

How to ask the right question and make the right contact

As an SME, you can draw on knowledge in a university to fix a problem, pull in an expert, explore a new line of business, test an idea or open up a market. Who exactly do you ask though? And what do you tell them? It can be harder than you think.

If you have a clear spec, then you can probably track down the kind of expert you need through a university's online directory. Alternatively talk to your trade association or chamber of commerce. Or work through one of the knowledge transfer networks (KTN) run by the Technology Strategy Board.

Then send them a summary of how you would like them to help. When it works, this approach is fast and efficient. Most universities have a central email address with recipients ready to turn round these kinds of enquiry.

But often universities find these emails hard to fathom. Databases of expertise are great if you know exactly what you are looking for. Most SMEs don't. In the thick of running a business, it can be hard to see the wider picture and figure out the real question.

Inevitably, you are bounded by your own experience. It helps to have an intelligent interface. So my advice is to pick up the phone. A five-minute call is usually more productive than a long, intricate email. As an enterprise, you will rarely, if ever, talk to a university. Whereas, universities are constantly in touch with SMEs and have spent 20 years learning how to find the right focus.

Your expectations

In approaching a university, it helps to understand what it actually offers. You might like to think it is an agency within the government's infrastructure for business support. In fact, universities are autonomous charitable institutions whose primary role is research and education. So for basic advice on how to run your business, you should probably start at your chamber of commerce.

For queries on accessing talent, just about any SME could contact a university. On technical questions, the university will gravitate towards anyone who is creating new ideas or testing the boundaries. For academics to take time away from their core activities of research and teaching, it has to be a project that engages their interest.

One common mistake is a conviction that only research will find an answer. In fact, many queries can be resolved by an academic acting as a consultant, laying out all the options.

Better questions quicker

There is no standard format for organising how the transfer of knowledge is managed. Each university has evolved in its own distinctive way. However, many are now putting in place a structure that cuts out any layers and allows you to talk directly to each centre of expertise.

At Newcastle, for instance, each of the three main faculties has its knowledge transfer team, who know the particular characteristics of their academics and where their research is heading. In the life sciences, you tend to be at the pure end of the scientific spectrum. In engineering, you are closer to market. In each case, the goal is to be as responsive as possible when an enterprise raises a challenge.

Web tools

The principle of sourcing ideas from anywhere is now well established. Instead of just relying on their own research, leading innovators are directing resources techniques such as technology scouting, crowd sourcing, open competitions and patent mapping. For SMEs, as well, it opens up the possibility of bringing in technologies, although it can be a frustrating jungle in which to search. However, there are a number of online tools that can help you:

- find a solution for a specific technical problem
- find innovative technologies that could be translated into a product
- keep track of innovation activities in specific sectors
- monitor competitors.

Email alerts through search engines are a good starting point. More specialised listings of technologies include: www.intellectualproperty.net; www.yet2.com, www.innocentive.com and www.university-technology.com.

The knowledge transfer networks (KTNs) run under the auspices of the Technology Strategy Board can also be a good source. They are run around 19 specialised areas of technology such as biosciences, electronics, ICT and creative industries. Further details at: https://ktn.innovateuk.org/.

Patent searching

The idea of a patent is to reward innovators and give them a period of exclusivity. In return it is designed to put advances in technology into the public domain. By reading the document you gain an understanding of what an innovation does and how it works.

On free-to-use databases, you can search by your type of technology, by your sector of the market, by the name of a competitor or by a keyword. Any patents you retrieve will break down into three parts. An introduction gives you a steer on why an invention or modification moves beyond the state of the art. A description then explains how the product or the process works, which is often accompanied by drawings. Finally, a series of claims are made which define the legal scope of what the patent protects. The initial claim is generally the broadest and most significant. Later ones will be more specific and conditional.

As you read the document, make sure you are aware of its status. If it is a published application, its claims will appear to be broad. If it is a granted patent, then the patent examiner is likely to have insisted on tighter and longer definitions. Remember too that not all patents are active. You are free to use these.

Networks

Many of the best innovations are the result of a series of almost random connections. Anyone who tries to bring all these variables together without networks would find it a maddeningly complex task. In inspiring insights and lining up resources, both enterprises and universities have an interest in making new connections whether locally, nationally or internationally, or by profession or discipline.

Networks can play a valuable role in spanning the different mindsets between research and business, particularly when looking at how new technologies might evolve. Similarly, networks can speed up innovation by re-deploying resources and bringing in the right people.

Start-up networks

To bring together the key players that help start-up ventures the Bath Ventures Innovation Centre has established a series of networks in high-growth areas. They're all free to join and shamelessly celebrate entrepreneurialism and the challenge of creating new businesses. For microelectronics entrepreneurs, the Silicon South West Network (www.siliconsouthwest.co.uk) publishes a regular newsletter reporting on new company developments in the sector and holds networking meetings where it invites entrepreneurs and investors to come and present. Similarly the Low Carbon South West Network (www.lowcarbonsouthwest.co.uk) focuses on cleantech and environmental technology; openMIC (http://open-mic.org.uk/), the Mobile Innovation Camp, brings together mobile apps developers with some of the major corporates in the mobile market to discuss mutual opportunities. Finally the Assisted Living Action Network (www.assistedlivingaction.net) provides a regular meeting spot for those interested in developing business opportunities in medtech and the massive global market for assisted living technology for the ageing population.

Regional networks

Regionally, no list of networks would be complete without reference to the Cambridge Network (www.cambridgenetwork.co.uk) which was one of the first and remains one of the most successful entrepreneurs' networks with close links to the university. Also, Cambridge Wireless (www.cambridgewireless.co.uk) has an unbeatable national and international reputation for its work in developing and promoting the region's highly successful wireless and mobile sector. In the South West, the Bath & Bristol Enterprise Network (www.bristolenterprise.com) similarly provides a regional focus for entrepreneurs and entrepreneurial academics to meet, mix and make the connections that will lead to the creation of new businesses.

9

Culture and priorities

When competing for a university's attention, four particular words make you stand out. So be sure to drop them into what you say about yourself

Put the right question to the right academic in the right way and the results can transform your business. In solving today's challenges, you can draw on a deep reserve of knowledge. Academics spend their lives exploring the limits of the possible. They will have a good sense of what research has already been conducted, what more needs to be done and how you can start pulling together a solution.

The danger is that your query can easily be lost. At any one time, commercial teams at universities are likely to have dozens of external requests for grants to develop ideas.

To access the university and all it can offer, you cannot just treat it as a convenient way of outsourcing your research. You have to gain a sense of its culture and its priorities.

To catch the interest of a busy academic audience, four words in particular might work in your favour: impact, discovery, challenge and data.

- **Impact.** Academics are living in a new world in which the criteria for funding their future research are no longer just based on its originality, but on the economic and social impact it makes. So spell out where your query might lead and who it might affect.

- **Discovery.** Rather than just asking a university to run a few tests on your early-stage idea, explain how it has the potential for turning into a breakthrough. Academics are in the business of discovery. If you can catch their imagination, they will run the tests as a matter of course, as well as writing letters of support and directing you towards potential sources of funding.

- **Challenge.** The world of innovation is being driven by cross-disciplinary attempts to find solutions to major public challenges, such as climate change and the ageing population. Many universities are now re-organising themselves as a matrix in which traditional faculties on one axis are cut across by five to six major challenges on another. So make sure you say how you fit into the wider picture and how you might attract funding from government bodies, such as the Technology Strategy Board.

- **Data.** Researchers almost always have a craving for real-life data. They might have the apparatus and know-how, but they are further from the direct experience and observation of how a problem manifests itself than you. If you can collect your findings and information in a form that can be analysed, your attractions as a partner can soar.

By highlighting how you can contribute to meeting academic priorities, you can start opening doors in the university. Culturally, you might still feel at a distance. Universities are naturally more in tune with corporates. They both move at a considered pace and any dialogue tends to be conducted between specialist researchers.

As a smaller company, you will be more commercially focused and will be looking for solutions in the here and now, rather than following speculative lines of inquiry. So how might you get yourself noticed? Three words come into play this time: access, profile, position.

- **Access.** Make a virtue of being small and close to market. Tell researchers that instead of sitting in a remote corner of a science park playing second fiddle, they will have direct access to the top of your company on a primary strategic issue that has every chance of being rapidly transferred into use. Equally, say upfront if your research partner has a chance of ending up in a senior role in your company within the next couple of years. A professor might be interested in joining your board, for instance, and an up-and-coming doctoral student could end up as your technical director in two years. Both are unlikely outcomes at your larger competitor.

- **Profile.** The demand for scientific and engineering talent is so high that you have to make your mark early. So sponsor prizes and competitions at the start of the academic year. Perhaps offer work experience and run placements as well. You will then be recognised when you want to bring in a researcher to your business.

- **Position.** Project yourself as an innovative venture and a potential partner for the university. Future rounds of research funding, such as the EU's Horizon 2020, are deliberately geared towards reviving industry through the most dynamic source of future wealth and jobs: SMEs. If you build the right relationship with a university, you could well find yourself part of a publicly funded programme to which you would never have previously had access.

However good your technical and operational capabilities, your chances of winning a slot on a public programme spot will be significantly less if you fail to express yourself in the terms that a university understands and that enable it to appreciate how you fit into the wider academic picture.

10

Intellectual property and the ownership of ideas

The IP culture within universities is evolving rapidly, giving more scope to negotiate a creative use of any commercial rights

The combination between a university's specialist knowledge and an enterprise's dynamic execution is a powerful source of innovation. By forging connections and partnerships, you can take the lead in your market, rather than trying to catch up. Yet the potential in such collaborations often falls short because of misunderstandings about who owns the intellectual property in the results and how these commercial rights can best be managed.

IP culture

As an enterprise, you are used to being black and white in your agreements. You expect to exercise control over any new features or points of difference you take to market. For the university, a duty to publish the results and educate its students runs alongside any commercial imperative.

However, the management of IP within universities is evolving rapidly. Professional teams are now usually in place at each of the three main stages of commercialising a technology: sourcing ideas, finding a path to market and negotiating transactions.

Academics are encouraged to make an early disclosure of any discoveries, so the release of any results can be sequenced with maintaining confidentiality before any IP is secured. Financially, any returns are usually split three ways between the academic, the department and the university. Just as important for most academics is the chance to demonstrate the impact of their work.

Patents remain the principal currency by which fundamental science is translated into the market, although an academic's know-how and expertise can be just as valuable in the eventual commercial outcome.

Conventionally, a university's IP then reaches the market through two main routes. Licences can bring the fastest results without much upfront cost. Spin-outs are usually for unproven, but potentially disruptive, technologies that are funded within a standalone structure.

Universities are increasingly open to how their IP is exploited. As many as half of their patents are filed by their industrial partners, usually in return for committing to fund research programmes. More experimentally, other forms of engagement are now being deployed:

- **pre-competitive IP is being generated within research groups in which industry sets challenges for academics: all the results are shared in common and each business has an option on any subsequent IP**

- **similarly, entrepreneurs are being asked to screen research proposals from faculties, commenting on what might work best commercially and what they might like to pursue within their own business**

- **academics' proposals are being circulated on open innovation networks in the crowd with an invitation to comment: anyone who is interested can then view the work confidentially**

- **through risk-sharing, smaller companies might be able to offset their initial costs against future earnings on any IP that is created.**

These techniques are designed to align more research more closely with demand and to operate in more open partnerships to define what IP might be possible. As universities become a more integral part of the whole innovation system, they are looking to build in as much value as they can to any ideas and to focus their IP on what business requires.

Collaborative models

The process of turning a raw piece of research into a ready-for-market application is one of the toughest challenges in business. When managed well, a portfolio of IP in the form of patents, trademarks, copyright, designs, domains and know-how can:

- **put you ahead of the market**
- **lock in a commercial advantage**
- **prevent anyone adopting your approach**
- **give you the freedom to operate**
- **let you charge a premium.**

However, misunderstandings can easily occur. Before everyone starts to ring-fence their IP, it is best to work out the interests of the various partners.

To speed up this process, the Intellectual Property Office has created a series of models and templates, which you can download for free (see Appendix 5).

None of these agreements will capture all of the particular features of any one project, but they do give you a basis on which to negotiate, allowing you to focus on the main sticking points. Agreements that once took months to finalise can now be put together in a matter of days.

To get you up to speed, an interactive decision guide clarifies your stance towards three underlying questions that will determine the nature of your relationship. Who is going to own and use the IP? Who is paying for the research? How are the results going to be used for academic purposes?

You will then be directed towards one of five model agreements. The first three models cover initial lines of inquiry in which the university holds the IP and an enterprise gains varying degrees of exclusivity to exploit it. The fourth and fifth models cover deeper collaboration which relies on technical and financial input from the enterprise. The fourth model is widely used: the enterprise gains the IP, but the university has the right to use it for non-commercial purposes. The fifth model covers contract research, where the university cannot use the results without permission.

In practice, enterprises often approach universities with queries for research, which turn out to be consultancy assignments. No new knowledge is being created and the academic prepares a report on the options that an enterprise has. A template is also available on the Intellectual Property Office's website, www.ipo.gov.uk.

Find the right path to market

The Intellectual Property Office has produced an online tool that is designed to help anyone with an idea to put their commercial thoughts in order. It is designed for those who understand the technical aspects of their IP deeply, but are looking for guidance on how to turn it into a business plan.

You are asked a series of stage questions. After checking the status of your IP, it explores your options for exploiting these rights. Are you going to use your own resources to build a business? Do you need a partner to capture the full potential of your idea? Or does it make sense to sell a licence and earn a stream of royalties?

In each case, you are taken down a logical path. Questions are strategic at first. In which markets do you want to be? What skills do you need? Do you have the cash to make it happen? What happens if anything goes wrong? How quickly are competitors going to respond?

You will then be asked a series of more specific questions about your IP. If you are going to do a deal, who will end up owning the IP and who has the rights to any follow-ups? What happens when someone challenges you? How do you divide up the money?

The idea is that you can test a series of scenarios, before you start talking to anyone more formally. Published under the title "Licensing your IP", the tool involves 20–25 questions and takes about an hour to complete.

www.ipo.gov.uk/iphealthcheck

Sticking points

In dealing with a university, it is always best to be clear about who exactly owns the IP on their side. As an employer, the university will normally expect to own the IP that its academics and graduates create in the course of their research. Undergraduates, who are paying for their courses, are generally free to exploit their own ideas. But take care to track down anyone else who might have a claim: is a corporation sponsoring any programmes? Is there a visiting fellow who works at another university? You do not want any surprises later.

As an SME, your collaborations will normally be one-offs, while you continue to run the rest of your business. Naturally, you will be concerned about injecting funds into any existing IP. Similarly, the university will want to retain a right to its own background technology. One answer is to identify any existing IP then license it to each other. Your priority will normally be on having clear access to any foreground IP; the university will want to retain the rights in any background research.

Similarly, confidentiality can cause difficulties. For enterprises, it is unreasonable to put a blanket on the whole university. Instead, it makes more sense to specify what discretion you expect from those who are working with you directly. You will also have to agree how and when any papers can be published.

IP tends to be a snapshot of an idea at a single point in time. Ideally, you want to make sure that you can continue to access all the knowledge and experience that sits around it. In any case, you want to be clear about who has the rights to follow up any of the results of your research in future. In particular, you would like to know if an academic subsequently unearths a hidden gem.

One tempting route to keep the project moving is to agree to joint ownership of any IP you create. It might work, but more usually it stores up trouble for later. If you both have a say in how the IP is going to be used, you can easily block yourselves out.

It is almost always better to attempt to construct win–win partnerships by recognising any differences in advance. Once the IP takes off, you can focus on creating a long-running source of competitive advantage and planning your future growth, rather than having to open a new round of negotiations.

Intellectual
Property
Office

Working with businesses and universities to harness the value of their Intellectual Property

To find out how we can help your business or university harness the value of Intellectual Property please visit:

**IP for business - www.gov.uk/government/publications/
intellectual-property-for-business**

**IP for universities - www.gov.uk/government/publications/
intellectual-asset-management-for-universities**

ntellectual
Property
Office

he Intellectual Property Office (IPO)

e role of the IPO is to develop and regulate an Intellectual Property (IP) system that encourages ovation and creativity, balances the needs of consumers and users, promotes strong and mpetitive markets and is the foundation of the knowledge-based economy.

e IPO carries out a range of activities to promote the value of IP and to provide advice and pport to businesses and universities seeking to maximise the value of their IP. By emphasising e value of collaborative working, we also seek to support businesses and universities in making e of each other's strengths and capitalising on their IP.

Intellectual Asset Management for Universities

The 'Intellectual Asset Management for Universities' guide aims to help senior managers in universities set strategies to optimise the benefits of the IP created by their staff and students. It encourages these decision makers to develop collaborative and contract research policies so that IP issues can be identified at an early stage, optimising the benefits of their IP.

Lambert Toolkit

The Lambert toolkit has been developed for businesses and universities that wish to undertake collaborative research projects with the aim of maximising innovation. The toolkit provides a set of model contracts, a decision guide and extensive educational resources and aims to help users conduct effective negotiations in public-private sector collaborative research. The toolkit is being updated by a practitioner group which includes representatives from different universities, businesses and technology sectors.

IP for Business

IP for Business is a range of online support tools to help SMEs and advisors identify, protect, use and grow their IP. It is made up of five individual yet complementary tools:

- IP Basics – A series of free business owner's guides to understanding IP.
- IP Equip – A free, interactive e-learning tool to help users identify assets which may be protected by IP rights.
- IP Equip app – A free app available for iOS and Android devices, offering IP information at your fingertips.
- IP Health Check – A free online tool to help businesses assess, identify and add value to their IP.
- IP Master Class – A popular accredited course on IP for business professionals which can be completed face to face or online.

Fast Forward Competition

Over the last four years the IPO has awarded £2.7 million in funding to 44 projects seeking to improve the management of intellectual property in Knowledge Exchange (KE) through its Fast Forward competition. This competition encourages universities to work with businesses and local communities to develop innovative KE practices, creating new companies and services which have benefited the UK economy and society.

Intellectual Property Office

CASE STUDY
IPO support for Bloodhound@University

The IPO's Fast Forward competition has provided funding to 44 innovative projects which improve the management of Intellectual Property in Knowledge exchange with £2.7 million in funding over four years.

Bloodhound@University is one such project and supports the university level activities of the Bloodhound SSC (Super Sonic Car) project. The groundbreaking Bloodhound SSC project aims to design, build and run a Mach 1.4 (1000mph) world land speed record car and is working to raise engagement with STEM (Science, Technology, Engineering and Mathematics) subjects at all levels of the education spectrum – from primary school to university.

Uniquely BloodhoundSSC shares data from the designing, building, testing and running of the car to provide unprecedented access to teachers, lecturers, pupils and students. University of the West of England (UWE) leads a network of universities who are using material from BloodhoundSSC in support of undergraduate teaching, postgraduate development work and PhD level studies.

The team have established a knowledge portal called the 'K-Box' based on data, know-how and expertise captured from the Bloodhound design team. This is now fully integrated into the main Bloodhound website, where users can access educational resources freely and explore wider subjects related to the programme. The project has also provided support for adoption and promotion of Additive Manufacturing (3D printing), an emerging 'Green Technology'. Additive Manufacturing is not well known outside aerospace and motorsport but Bloodhound will use this technology on the car and then demonstrate its capabilities to a global audience.

Subsequent to the IPO project supported work, UWE has secured additional further funding from EPSRC to support the development of specific teaching case studies for use at universities and colleges. Another way in which the work supported by IPO funding has continued beyond the funded period is the detailed design and manufacture of the drivers steering yoke.

An initial ergonomic project was undertaken at UWE with a group of Product Design students who worked with Andy Green, the driver, on the shape / form of cockpit and steering yoke. Proposed solutions were used to form a more detailed functional prototype over the following 12 months through a student placement with the engineering team. 18 months later, the engineering team needed some further user and performance requirements factored into the yoke design.

Working with academics at Lancaster University a two week design project was set for a group of 30 Year IV MEng Engineering students. The brief was centred on ensuring the yoke would be stiff enough to meet the loads imposed by the driver/run - but at the same time reducing the weight - a classic design optimisation/ trade study problem. The students devised 25 different topological solutions that had been designed/modelled in 3D CAD. Harnessing the "crowd source" effect of the student groups in this way delivered, in two weeks, a group of solutions equivalent to over two years of engineering work complete with finely detailed CAD and load models, allowing a step change in the design and structure of the yoke.

11

Grant funding

Experts for free? Universities give you a series of stepping stones to finance the development of an idea

Pronunciation is one of the trickiest challenges for the world's two billion learners of English as a second language. All those irregularities, inflections and idiosyncrasies. Yet teachers rarely have time to practise with their pupils. The focus is more on grammar and vocabulary.

So could you put together some speech recognition with a programme that automatically corrects words when they come out wrong? And what about giving it an element of fun by making it visual and including some games?

It was an idea that initially occurred six years ago to Colin Hamilton, a website manager in Glasgow, while he was running a voluntary class for lifelong learners. It was an experience that set him thinking about how to extend the use of educational technology to help with illiteracy, special needs and basic English.

After a conversation with Education Scotland, he opted to focus first on those trying to learn English. At this point, he could have opted to pitch for venture capital and leave his job, but felt that the idea was still too early stage and that he could end up giving away three-quarters of his company, Micro-phonics.

Students participating in a pilot for Micro-phonics run by the University of Glasgow

Instead, he has taken a different path, raising a succession of grants to refine his idea through Scotland's universities:

- he has used a series of innovation vouchers, worth £3,000–£5,000, to investigate different technical challenges

- he won an award for £2,000 from the business angels at Strathclyde in a competition for the best pitch

- he is just completing a 2½ year pilot of his programme with an academic team funded through the University of Glasgow

- and he has put together a proposal for a PhD to research rhythm in language which will run through the University of Glasgow, although Hamilton will have first call on the commercial use of any intellectual property.

Individually, these grants might appear to amount to "dribs and drabs" but together they have let Hamilton assemble a team of experts essentially for free to verify his idea to the point where it has became a finalist in the British Council's awards for educational technology and will be ready for launch in Scotland later this year, then the rest of the UK, before being distributed globally through Amazon.

Through a grant from Scottish Enterprise, Hamilton is currently working on his marketing to heads of schools and is about to consult Scottish Development International on how to price his product in different markets.

"There are always pockets of money somewhere," says Hamilton. "Once you make an enquiry, universities will start looking at what grants they can raise against it. On your first project, it might be an innovation voucher. Otherwise they will find another form of funding."

In putting together his latest proposal for a PhD to be funded by grant from a research council, he has worked closely with his academic partners at the University of Glasgow. "You don't need to do all the legwork yourself," he says. "Find yourself a strong academic partner. They will then make it happen and find the funding themselves."

Stepping stones

Professor Andrew Pollard at the Caparo Innovation Centre at the University of Wolverhampton is well used to helping enterprises construct a series of stepping stones to help them offset the costs of innovation.

The first step he recommends is to map out how much cash you are going to require – and when. "Once you have your analysis, you can think about how you are going to manage your outgoings, as well as how you might defer them," he says.

"Grants are less freely available than they were five years ago, but it is worth thinking broadly about how you might use them . A university is likely to be your first approach, but local authorities might help in deferring your rates and charities might be interested in an aspect of your innovation."

So what might be available through the University of Wolverhampton? Currently, it is running four support schemes up to June 2015, each backed by European Regional Development Funding:

- **Innovation First:** over two days, you can map out what technologies you might deploy in your company

- **Innovative Product Support Service:** you can access five days of technical support: for instance, you might opt to design a 3D model; or you could ask for an electronic specification for a circuit board; or you could have an IP strategy written before deciding how to file for any intellectual property

- **I-UEN (Innovation University Enterprise Network):** another five days can be spent on preparing for a potential collaboration with a larger company or engaging with them through open innovation. You can get help to hone your pitch, put your market research into a coherent form and set out your proposition to a potential partner

- **Technology & Innovation Futures:** offers a 50% grant towards the cost of work by University specialists to develop designs and prototypes, which can be claimed once the work is completed.

Each scheme has its own criteria, of course, but are all targeted at smaller companies. In the EU's next funding round, Horizon 2020, this emphasis on innovation and enterprise is likely to be even stronger in supporting collaborative research.

Types of funding

Grants for SMEs can be found in numerous different guises, but essentially break down into three types: early-stage and follow-on support for investigating an idea; the transfer of knowledge and the mobility of talent; and research programmes.

Early-stage and follow-on support for investigating ideas

In Scotland, Wales and Northern Ireland, official schemes to encourage local SMEs to engage with universities run under the title of "innovation vouchers". You are given a credit, channelled through your academic partner, for running a research or consultancy assignment with the university. The schemes are designed to encourage collaborations that might not otherwise happen. Normally, you are expected to cover half the costs.

A fresh source of funding has emerged for smaller companies with ideas in science, engineering and technology. From April 2011, three types of grant became available from the Technology Strategy Board: up to £25,000 to prove a market; up to £100,000 to prove an idea; and up to £250,000 to create a prototype.

This R&D scheme from the Technology Strategy Board replaces what the regional development agencies used to offer. The scheme will run alongside existing programmes in Scotland, Wales and Northern Ireland.

The transfer of knowledge and the mobility of talent

In working with universities to find new solutions and make improvements, Knowledge Transfer Partnerships are the flagship programme for bringing in the best minds to your company. Typically, a graduate will come and work for you under a senior academic's supervision for one to three years. A new product, a new service or a new process might be the result.

Two-thirds of the cost is met through a grant from the Technology Strategy Board in recognition of the value that is created for the university in undertaking these kinds of collaborative project. As an SME, you pay for the rest, although you have the chance to review your involvement after three months.

For SMEs, there is an option to run shorter programmes of 10 to 40 weeks. After a recent confirmation that the scheme will continue as an integral part of the government's commitment to accelerating innovation, SMEs can also qualify to pay 25% instead of 33% of the cost.

Other programmes can be run directly through the UK's seven research councils. Although their primary role is to fund the work of academics, they also run schemes to fund the placement of students and academics within your company.

All offer CASE studentships (Collaborative Awards in Science and Engineering), for instance, which support research for doctorates being carried out in collaboration with a business partner. In return for setting the direction of the research, you will typically be expected as a partner to cover a third of the costs, which can total £70,000 over three years.

In universities in Wales, a series of four additional schemes run to encourage the mobility of knowledge between universities and business.

Collaborative research

To develop key technologies or meet challenges in public policy, government bodies run competitions to find potential partners and match their funding in finding solutions. Priorities are identified under the auspices of the Technology Strategy Board, which draws together a programme in partnership with all the main players in the market. It then launches an open competition to search for potential partners, who are almost always expected to work in collaboration. To accelerate the creation and adoption of ideas, the TSB recognises that it is better to pool knowledge and co-operate in networks of value, so it actively encourages the involvement of SMEs, whose focus and adaptability often puts them ahead of the game.

Under the Small Business Research Initiative, the TSB enables SMEs to bid to develop innovations for challenges identified in the public sector. If accepted, you are typically awarded up to £100,000 to prove within six months whether your idea is technically feasible. The most promising candidates might then receive £1m over two years to run demonstrations.

Even in the EU's flagship programme for building up cross-border research, Framework 7, which is running a 50bn euro programme over seven years, recognition is given to the ingenuity and creativity of SMEs. A target has been set of directing 15% of those funds towards them. More details can be found through the TSB or through knowledge transfer offices.

Funding bodies

Technology Strategy Board

The TSB is the national agency for innovation that was created in 2007 to assist business across the UK to develop technology from concept to the market. It works in close collaboration with over 150 different institutions in research, including nearly all the universities. Its budget of £300m has been increased for 2015–16 by £185m.

Funds are awarded competitively on the basis of excellence regardless of where a business is located. In amount, 30% goes to its partners in the research base, such as universities, and 60% is linked to projects that involve collaboration with the research base.

Among its programmes, it spends:

- **£3.5m on innovation vouchers targeted at SMEs to investigate their ideas through a university**

- **£36.4m on a series of grants for SMEs to take an idea from concept to prototype**

- **£16.9m on a scheme for postgraduates to transfer their knowledge and apply their skills**

- **£172.9m on collaborative R&D projects, which range in value from £10,000 to £100m+. Many appear as open competitions designed to fast-track the development of solutions.**

Research councils

The UK's seven research councils span all fields of knowledge. Together they invest £3bn a year in maintaining the UK's world-class reputation for research. In pursuit of excellence with impact, each council runs a range of initiatives to engage business and de-risk innovation. Research councils currently have direct links with 2,500 companies and a fifth of all PhDs formally collaborate with business. They are also investing in innovation hubs to speed up the transfer of knowledge and in larger campuses for science and innovations, such as the one at Harwell, which is now an enterprise zone where 4,500 people work in over a hundred different organisations. The seven research councils are:

1. **Biotechnology and Biological Sciences Research Council**

2. **Economic and Social Research Council**

3. **Engineering and Physical Sciences Research Council**

4. Medical Research Council

5. Natural Environment Research Council

6. Science and Technologies Facilities Council

7. Arts and Humanities Research Council

Higher education funding councils

The funding councils award grant to universities on the basis of regular reviews of their research. HEFCE, the funding council for England, for instance, currently puts £6.5bn a year into 130 universities and 124 FE colleges. The size of these grants is determined by a series of regular reviews. In the one currently underway (the research excellence framework), quality is still assessed against traditional academic yardsticks, but a new element is being introduced as well. The impact that research makes on the economy and on society now accounts for 20% of any award. For academics everywhere, an incentive is being created to find applications for their work in the real world.

Each of the four funding councils in England, Scotland, Wales and Northern Ireland has also played an instrumental role in building up the capacity within universities to engage with business. HEFCE, for instance, is currently committed to providing £160m a year to give universities the scope to develop the commercial dimension of their activities, either through knowledge or enterprise education.

Local economic partnerships

LEPs were created in 2010 throughout England to promote local growth and take the lead in drawing up a strategic plan. Existing mechanisms to support economic development continued in Scotland, Wales and Northern Ireland. England's 39 LEPs are guaranteed £2bn a year in funding from the government and are being allocated €6.2bn during the course of 2014–20 by the European Structural and Investment Fund: €1bn of these funds are targeted at innovation.

Universities sit on two-thirds of LEPs' boards and often play an instrumental role in their activities. In a recent review of collaboration between universities, Sir Tim Wilson, former vice-chancellor of Hertfordshire University comments: "universities are key players in the supply chain for research, innovation and skills: they should be at the heart of a LEP".

In a follow-up report on universities and growth, the chief executive of GlaxoSmithKline, Sir Andrew Witty, recommends that a large share of the LEPs' €1bn budget should be directed towards universities and research, encouraging every innovative SME in their area to engage with a university.

The EU

The EU runs two major programmes in pursuits of its strategy for more smart, sustainable and inclusive growth by 2020: Horizon 2020 and its regional development fund.

At €77bn over seven years to 2020, Horizon 2020 represents the world's largest research programme. As well as reinforcing Europe's scientific excellences, its goals are to speed up innovation and encourage the participation of SMEs.

Overall, 20% of the funds are expected to flow to SMEs. The intent is to focus on "close-to-market" support so research is profitably translated into innovation.

Usually, SMEs will take part as part of a consortium and many universities are currently screening who they might recruit as potential partners.

In addition, a new "SME instrument" is being introduced to fill gaps in funding for early-stage, high-risk projects with an EU dimension. Previous EU schemes are being combined in the hope of making it easier to access funding.

For 2014–20, the European Regional Development Fund has a budget €351bn to improve the capability of all regions to compete and to attract investment. According to Dr David Bembo at the University of Cardiff and chair of AURIL (Association for University Research and Industry Links), it has a particularly strong role to play in regions where corporate R&D is relatively low and which rely heavily on SMEs for growth.

Innovation is one of the programme's declared objectives and the allocation funds to support SHEs has been doubled to €140bn in the years through to 2020. As significant local economic players, universities are one of the principal channels through which these funds are likely to flow.

The Future Factory at Nottingham Trent University is one example of an ERDF initiative through which SMEs are supported in creating and designing more sustainable solutions. Another is a scheme through the University of Liverpool that runs a free recruitment service for SMEs to take on graduates, so keeping them within the local economy.

12

Locate on-site

The benefits of locating a business within a university's innovation or enterprise centre

The space between a university and the market can be an attractive base for a spin-out or for your own start-up. Within an innovation or enterprise centre, you can operate on flexible terms until you are ready to grow. You can keep yourself up to speed with the latest thinking in your field. You can bring in specialists. You can use state-of-the-art facilities to test your ideas. You can join a cluster of like-minded enterprises. You can call on business advice and support. You can put yourself in front of investors within the university's network.

At some universities such as Coventry, which occupies a 60-acre area in the middle of the city on the site of the old Rolls-Royce plant, you can move from early stage to full operation without leaving the campus. At others, facilities are more spread out, but can still put you on an escalator to growth.

The experience is quite different from a serviced office, says Margaret Henry at Oxford Innovation, which accommodates 500 enterprises in 20 different centres across the country. "They are meant to be about collaboration and growth, encouraging you to make contacts and raise finance. We are deliberately looking to foster a community of entrepreneurs."

Virtual tenants and hot desking

To get you started and to test the water, you can adopt a virtual presence in an innovation centre or technology park. For about £100 a month, you will be given an address, someone will answer your calls, you will be able to drop into the centre, you can hold a meeting, you can book a room and you will be invited to networking events. For perhaps £200, you will be able to use a desk for a few days a month.

Incubators and innovation centres

Incubators tend to operate within the university. Innovation centres are run outside. Both offer space and support on flexible terms. Rather than committing to a lease for a number of years, you take out a licence month by month. It is easy to scale back, if your idea fails to meet expectations, or move upstairs into a bigger office when you pick up speed.

What might an incubator look like? At the University of Manchester, there are now five. The first, opened in 1999 next to the faculty of medicine and life science, is for biotech ventures. "It is designed as a space where you can circulate and meet," says Tony Walker, Director of Enterprise and Business Development at UMIP (University of Manchester Intellectual Property), "and where you can use test equipment which would otherwise be prohibitively expensive."

The rent at such centres tends to be just above the local commercial rate, because so many extra growth services come as part of the package. You will be able to ask questions of a business adviser, for instance. Oxford Innovation might also find you a coach and help put together your senior team.

Enterprise centres and grow-on space

Currently, 60% of the occupants at Manchester's biotech incubator are university spin-outs and 40% are external ventures. Once they have proved they have a market, they can move into a grow-on space within the "health corridor" that the university is creating. "It is just opposite the teaching hospital," says Walker, "so they are well placed to start conducting clinical trials."

On the campus at Coventry, you can move into similar enterprise centres, depending on the industry in which you operate. For product designers, there is a specialist hub, which houses Tata Design Technologies, part of the group that now owns Jaguar Land Rover, as well as part of the faculty. Or there are similar institutes in areas such as health, computer games, creative industries and construction, which operate as a halfway house between research and industry.

Business and science parks

Once an enterprise starts to become operational, it will want to fit out its own space and have the security of a lease well into the future. At Coventry, you can stay on campus and move into the Innovation Village, which offers a choice within eight large buildings.

At Manchester, the next natural step is the science park, which is part-owned by the university. Over the last 25 years, it has grown into eight purpose-built buildings, which house over a thousand people in all areas of economic activity.

"We want to grow and retain the knowledge base," says Tony Walker. "Across all of our spaces for innovation, we have a revolving door, creating room for growth for smaller companies who want to collaborate with the university."

13

Venture funding

Universities occupy a pivotal role in unearthing promising ideas and finding the capital to support them

A decade ago, universities tended to draw on investors within half an hour's drive of the university. Now they are casting a much wider creative and financial net to attract "smart money" into early-stage technology.

"We have an open mind of how to put together a package," says Tom Hockaday, chief executive of Isis Innovation, the company that was created to commercialise technology from the University of Oxford in 1987. "For us, it is the art of the possible. We are unlikely to have the luxury of having 10 offers from which to choose. It is a question of putting together a strong offering, then talking to the broadest possible long list."

He sees his role as assembling the team and keeping it together. "It has always been a three-dimensional challenge. We connect the world of research with the world of commerce and the world of finance. Now we have a fourth dimension, as investments start to come in from China, Hong Kong and the Middle East."

Not all universities can draw on the reputation or resources of Oxford, but they are still exploring all the options that are available to them. Coventry, for instance, runs an equity committee, on which entrepreneurs, investors and bankers sit alongside the vice-chancellor and the university's director for enterprise. Together they screen any ideas that are coming through the university with a view to plugging them into funding networks within the West Midlands.

Finding the backing for such early-stage ventures is never easy. The risks are too high for bank finance, of course, and conventional venture capital investors generally prefer ideas that have already reached the market. Unless they fall for a fad or jump on a bandwagon, investors are wary about committing to technologies that they do not understand. In raising the funds to bring such ideas to markets, universities have a series of options which they can bring into play.

Seed capital

To prove a concept or build a demonstrator, universities often invest amounts of £5,000 to £25,000 from funds that they manage themselves. The University of Manchester, for instance, has a £3.2m line of finance to help it jump through the main hurdle in technology transfer: to develop a prototype with a robust proprietary position and a credible strategy.

"We like to have ready-to-hand funding for proof of principle and proof of market to meet our deal flow projections," says Clive Rowland, chief executive of UMI[3], the university's innovation group. "We can then get projects launched which would otherwise not see the light of day."

Similarly, Oxford has two funds for testing inventions and Coventry now has a facility through the Higher Education Innovation Fund to put £5,000 into proof of concept.

Spin-out capital

Once verified, an idea is now in a much better position to attract larger amounts of money. The conventional route is to raise £500,000 from private investors, or angels as they are commonly known, before approaching venture capitalists for subsequent rounds of £2m, then £5m.

At Oxford the main forum for raising this money is the Isis Angel Network, when a room of up to 150 potential investors gathers to screen four to five proposals. Typically, they used to be local entrepreneurs who had sold their own ventures and were ready to put their funds and expertise back into early-stage ventures. Now they are a much wider mix. Together with high-net-worth individuals from China, private equity is represented within the network as well.

Sometimes, one investor will take the lead and pull together a consortium, or Isis will pull together a group of between three and 20 individuals. Sometimes, Hockaday and his colleagues will be approached by an intermediary on behalf of an international investor.

The angel market

Such angel networks are usually managed by companies such as Oxford Innovation. Operating on a national basis, its main network raises investments between £100,000 and £2m. For angels, who are interested in higher risk at the early stage, it runs a network for concept funding between £25,000 and £100,000.

Such support for innovative ventures is about to be strengthened by the government's new co-investment fund. Once a venture has a commitment from its angels, it can draw down a similar amount, so doubling the size of the funds it has raised. A similar scheme runs in Scotland (the Scottish Co-Investment Fund).

Leapfrog capital

On this ladder of finance, the danger is that seed investors can fall off and make less money than they should. The risks are relatively high and the funds are relatively small, so they can easily find themselves diluted and replaced.

Ideally, you want spin-outs to have enough resources at their disposal to scale up. At Manchester, the solution has been to create a £32m fund, 10% of which goes on proof of concept and the rest then follows in subsequent rounds. Both the spin-out and the investor gain scale and continuity.

In the Midlands, investors can access a similar source of funding through the Mercia Fund. It offers "pathfinder" grants of up to £250,000, which turn into equity or a royalty when the venture is launched. Mercia then makes a further equity investment in the normal way.

Corporate venturing, charitable grants

Private investors are not the only players at the early stage of spinning out ideas. Corporates, such as GSK and its SRI fund, will look at investing at the early stage. Many more, that are committed to speeding up their search for ideas through open innovation, are looking to give spin-outs some scale through revenue-sharing deals.

Other active participants in the market are charities. In healthcare, for instance, the Wellcome Trust acts as a major partner in bringing fundamental research closer to the market. Funds are rarely released directly as cash into your account. They are normally in the form of grants for programmes with conditions attached, often turning into a convertible loan when an idea is commercialised.

Smart money

"By definition, university companies are a long play," says Tom Hockaday. "Opportunities to make a quick return are limited. So we prefer active to passive money from those who have the experience of successfully growing companies themselves and who will put the effort into building the board."

Clive Rowland at Manchester puts it another way:

> "The trick for us is to identify the right sort of projects and weave in the investment, marketing and entrepreneurial expertise, then start to take a back seat so that the businesses can grow with the right sort of teams in place. Our job then is to go back into the university and assist the transfer of the next set of projects."

PART 3
Access to talent

14

Bring in an expert

As consultants, academics are often well placed to give you answers to bring you up to speed in resolving a testing challenge

When you are selling ice cream, it helps to know what your customers want and when. If you are folding metals in new ways, your performance has to be as precise as possible to interest buyers in aerospace and automotive. If you are building solar-powered lighting for use in countries such as Madagascar, you have to make your LED circuit durably rugged and reasonably priced.

In resolving any of these types of challenge, you can rely on your instincts to find a way of taking your business up a level. Or you could draw on the underlying science to verify the best way forward.

For ice cream, behavioural economics can give you a statistical breakdown of what customers expect. In folding metal, a mechanical engineer can create models for how your materials respond. For solar-powered LEDs, an energy specialist can test whether your circuit designs could work for the quarter of the world's population who cannot afford conventional sources of lighting.

Academics at institutions as august as Imperial College London are often readier to help you solve such technical and commercial challenges than you might expect. To justify their ranking as one of the world's top 10 universities, they are actively looking to infuse their research and teaching with real-life challenges.

For example, Dr Daniel Balint from Imperial's Department of Mechanical Engineering used his expertise in material deformation and mathematical modelling to help RoboFold improve the precision of their robotic manufacturing system that creates curved metal forms. This has allowed RoboFold to move into new markets such as aerospace and automotive.

At Imperial, you can draw on the knowledge of 3,000 researchers who are working across four main disciplines: engineering, medicine, natural science and business. As consultants, they are open to working on assignments that can vary in size from half a day's brainstorming to a multi-year project.

You might feel you have to go to the top and call on a leading professor. Often, it makes just as much sense to work with a postgrad researcher. All of them are experts in their field, putting them in a good position to review your options and check out your plans.

The outcome of any assignment nearly always depends on asking the right question in the first place. You might have a clearly formed idea of the outcome. Others often have less experience of how to define the scope of a project.

To facilitate engagements, Imperial Consultants (ICON) is the starting point for making any enquiries. They will help to define what you are actually asking and put you in touch with the right academic. In total, they are currently running around 500 projects, which vary in value from £1,000 to well over a million.

Since the early 1990s, Imperial Consultants has operated as a separate company, owned by Imperial. It now employs a team of 30 and generates revenues of £26m a year. The consultants on which it calls are academics and all its profits go back into funding future research within the university.

To let you make the most of your time with an academic, Imperial Consultants has standard sets of terms. If you are running a test in the wind tunnel, these might run to a couple of pages. If you are starting a year-long project, they will be longer and you will probably want to include some of your own conditions anyway.

Many of the smaller assignments revolve around seeking an independent scientific opinion on what a venture is proposing. Imperial's view carries significant weight, of course, although the college insists it cannot give any form of endorsement and will be scrupulous in how it reports the results, whether they make happy reading or not.

Some ventures opt for a rolling contract, under which they can call on a certain amount of scientific advice during the year. For any extra, they will then pay the daily rate.

The advantage of consultancy is that it usually represents the fastest and cleanest way of transferring knowledge. Any intellectual property generally rests with you as the client. The only exception is when Imperial has to bring in its own IP to give you an answer.

So on some projects, you will find everyone operating under confidentiality. You keep your IP secret; Imperial keeps theirs; everyone keeps a focus on proving the principle on which you hope to base your business.

"The focus of our academics might be on the future," says Rebecca Andrew at Imperial Consultants, "but their knowledge is right at the edge of their field, so you will always get the most up-to-date thinking and technologies coming through to solve problems faced today."

15

Workforce training

Universities are learning to design training for where and when companies want it

In a seminar you can pick up most of the risks you will encounter on a building site, but the implications will resonate with you more if you actually experience them for yourself. At Coventry University, you will now find yourself in front of a 180° wraparound simulator in which a series of accidents will happen, such as girders that come crashing down. You will then be put through your paces by a series of Shakespearean actors on release from Stratford-upon-Avon, posing as health-and-safety inspectors or aggrieved customers.

On the day-long course developed with the Chartered Institute of Building, your reactions are measured in real time and your performance is filmed to play back for review later. All being well, you will gain a certificate in project management from the university.

The chances of you retaining what you have learnt from such simulations developed by the university's Serious Games Institute is usually reckoned to be 80% higher than through more conventional days spent in a lecture hall.

"You are having to act on your feet, not just in the classroom," says Brian More at Coventry University Enterprises. "We tend to simulate real construction sites like Brindley Place in Birmingham, where you have to respond to real problems and manage your own time."

A similar course is being run for the fire service, in which everyone is put under the stress of an unfolding disaster to test how they are going to react. The university then follows up with courses in leadership and management.

In all its training for skills in the workplace, the university is seeking to adopt a more professional approach to competing in the market. Four years ago, it set up its own company, Acua Solutions, to package its capabilities in research and training into formats that were easier for companies to access.

"At Acua, the focus is on delivering training where and when a company wants it," says Brian More. "We work in all formats. It might be a conventional course on campus. We might come to you. It might be online. Probably, it will be a combination of all three."

A course can be structured as a formal qualification. Or it can be modular in format, allowing you to take a series of units that count towards a final result: 60 points for a certificate; 120 points for a postgraduate diploma; and 180 points for a degree.

Leadership and management is the area that tends to attract most interest, although the university has particular strengths in engineering design, IT programming and health care.

As well as corporates, such as Jaguar Land Rover, the university is developing capabilities within more and more SMEs, many on officially funded programmes. The European Regional Development Fund, for instance, supports Touch Digital, which is designed to bring SMEs up to speed as to how they can use digital technologies in their business.

As far as possible, Acua draws on the latest research from academics within their framework of "excellence with impact", which addresses major challenges within business and in society. One course that is currently developing is for architects and designers to give them an insight into the full potential of low-carbon buildings based on the work being undertaken in the university's centre of excellence.

For the academics, it can represent an attractive way of transferring their knowledge into use. Unlike spin-outs, which usually take time and require the adoption of a new commercial mindset, training is a natural extension of an academic's everyday activities in training and research.

Acua can also draw on the "extra skills" that the university is now teaching its students. Unlike 20 years ago, when a degree usually led to a permanent job, the average pattern for today's graduates is perhaps 20 different positions by their late 30s. Many will set up their own company, so the university is developing the capability for all of them to run their own business.

By drawing on this outward-looking learning culture, as well as the university's capabilities in research, Acua has grown the university's income from workforce training from a few hundred thousand four years ago to £5m. "Our goal," says More, "is to continue designing courses around what companies want."

Value of work-based learning for the employer

According to Professor Simon Roodhouse at Middlesex University, the value to the employer of work-based learning and accreditation can be summarised in the following ways:

- employees undertake real work in company projects which are of direct benefit to the organisation

- it realises the intellectual capital of the company

- it encourages self-confidence by recognising individual experience and accrediting it

- it provides a means of measuring the performance of externally purchased training programmes through assessment

- minimum loss of work time, it is not campus based

- increased loyalty results from the visible investment in the development of the workforce

- staff retention rates are improved and enhanced capabilities of existing workforce can help with recruitment, both as a means of attracting new employees, but also as a means of promoting from within the organisation

- organisations can work with a university to develop a tailor-made award which supports the individual professional development of employees but also reflects organisational priorities

- organisational and cultural change can be supported through work-based learning projects

- work-based learning is a means of addressing strategic business objectives and meeting an organisation's business plans

- employers and employees are in the driving seat taking control of their learning.

16

Live company projects

To bring in fresh thinking, give students a question to answer

When you are thinking about garden furniture, your eye may well be drawn to an unusual lounger in wide weave shaped like a tongue. Or if you have a small garden in town, you might have a look at a set of twisted table and stools.

Both are the result of a joint project at Birmingham City University driven by Hartman, a leading name in upmarket garden furniture. "We are not product designers, so we are always looking for new ideas," says Gina Hinde, the UK marketing manager at the company. "In the past, we have worked with Jamie Oliver and Kew Gardens on new lines. Sometimes these collaborations work. Sometimes they don't."

For Hartman, whose sales in the UK fluctuate between £8m and £12m, it is imperative to keep ahead in the competitive world of garden furniture. Its Dutch parent is a major player in Europe, but its designs in aluminium are less popular in the UK, which still prefers to stick to wood and weave when relaxing in the sun.

Last year, Hinde was looking for inspiration at the Interiors show at the National Exhibition Centre in Birmingham, when she came across the university's stand. Its two displays caught her imagination. First, students from the design school had produced a series of interpretations of how future trends might be realised at home and in the garden. Second, they had created designs for eight to 10 different companies.

The tongue lounger was designed by Justine Woolley and retails at £140

The twisted set was designed by Amit Fox and retails at £275

What were the chances of producing some ideas for Hartman? she wondered. "It would be great for us to work with some up-and-coming designers, who clearly had no fear in putting ideas out there."

For the university, it could mean giving students the chance to work on a real-life project to build up their portfolios and improve their chance of landing a job at the end of their three years.

After the Interiors show, Hinde followed up her interest and agreed to make Hartman's search for new ideas part of the following year's curriculum for students in their final year at the design school. In return, she agreed to put up £1,000 for the winning design and £500 for the runner-up, then take their ideas into production, sharing any intellectual property and paying the students a royalty on sales.

On the first day of term last year, 29 students went to Hartman's operation in Telford, where they were given a briefing on what was expected and given an insight into the process of how products reached the customer. "If we are manufacturing in China, we want to produce and transport our designs as efficiently as possible," says Hinde.

A few months later, the university put the results on display. "We were blown away. Everything was so professional. We were expecting to see line drawings, so the 3D designs and full-scale models came as a surprise.

"We were spoilt for choice," she says. "We would never have thought of some of the designs. It was great to work with students at the start of their careers, before they become jaded."

Hinde eventually whittled the submissions down to 10 and then asked everyone at Hartman to vote on their favourites. The winner was a large woven pod with a table inside, which is proving difficult to make, but will be launched next year. Two of the runners-up are already in the catalogue: the tongue lounger and the twisted set of table and stools.

Hinde was happy to repeat the experience with the next crop of students. "This year, we are setting a tighter brief. Previously, we asked for a family range, which was too broad."

As well as the one with Hartman, the university will be running eight to 10 other collaborations in design as part of its strategy to re-engineer the curriculum to include as much direct experience as possible. As well as garden furniture, the 120 students on the course will be working on ideas for flooring, wallpaper and lighting.

"We make these challenges a day-to-day part of the university," says Joanna Birch, head of enterprise development at Birmingham City. "Nothing runs in isolation. Consultancy, income generation, knowledge transfer, learning and research all sit together. By embedding them all in the existing system, we can keep our costs down to a minimum."

As well as designers, Birch, who joined the university after a career in pulling together all the elements for major property developments, is introducing this approach to all other academic disciplines, including law, education and the social sciences.

"It is all about speed," she says. "We are working on creating a system that can turn round opportunities quickly enough for business."

17

Short-term assignments

Interns? Placements? Part-timers? Graduates and students can offer great value in sorting out commercial and technical challenges for SMEs

Do you have a task that you should sign off but are struggling to find someone with the time? Perhaps you are under pressure to produce a carbon footprint or follow up a lead in a new market. Typically, you might pull someone off the frontline to have a go. They might spend an hour or two checking out your question on the first day, then leave it for a couple of weeks. It is a familiar scenario, when you are running a lean team and chasing business.

One alternative might be to bring in a graduate on a short-term assignment that might last from a couple of days to 12 months. Keele is one of many universities which has started running these kinds of programme for SMEs which are facing a one-off challenge.

Prompted by a local engineering practice, Wardell Armstrong, Keele launched Project Green with backing from HEFCE. As an SME, you could bring in a graduate for four to seven weeks at no cost to sort out an environmental issue, such as reducing waste, saving energy or complying with legislation. The university also ran a course to bring all the participants up to speed.

The results for both sides were surprisingly positive, reports Nadine Pendry, a manager at the university who is responsible for engagements with employers. "SMEs found that taking on a graduate fresh from university with no pre-conceptions really helps the business. You don't have to train them. Just give them a clear set of objectives and they will get their heads down. In a number of cases, savings of hundreds of thousands of pounds were made on energy bills."

For graduates, it offers a first step in their careers. Some have been offered extensions to their assignments, says Pendry. All of the others have been in a stronger position to apply for full-time jobs and to perform at interview. "Instead of saying what they could or would do, they can talk convincingly about what they have already done."

A follow-up project, Destination Green, has been launched. Academics at the university size up each challenge. A student then works on site for 14 weeks, paid £100 per week by the company and £250 through the university. A £1,500 voucher to run a short innovative project at the university is also part of the package for SMEs.

More broadly, under a scheme co-ordinated by Aston University, you can approach Keele with any kind of commercial or technical challenge. "We will produce a shortlist of three to four candidates for you to interview and employ directly," says Pendry. "The only condition is that you agree to pay them at least £6.90 an hour."

Keele is running another programme with Santander, the high-street bank. Under this collaboration, assignments will last 12 weeks and will be open to any challenges that a graduate could tackle for an SME.

So what are the options for bringing students or graduates into your business? An internship is the preferred route for graduates. At the University of Manchester, for instance, the careers office has a thousand students in their final year who are looking to work on short-term contracts.

No charge is made for any of the costs of recruitment, although employers are expected to pay interns at the going rate for graduates.

"When we are approached, we like to get inside the role. See what skills the business is actually looking for," says Anne Milligan, who leads the small business team in the careers and employability division at the University of Manchester.

"We then often write the job description and run an ad. We can even receive applications on behalf of the company, draw up a shortlist and help to arrange interviews."

Placements are designed for students during the course of their degree. Traditionally, they spent a year working in a business before returning to complete their degree. Few SMEs are able to plan as far in advance as a placement might require. One recent development might help. Placements are being split into a series of 6–8-week chunks, which can be agreed closer to when they are needed.

An alternative way to bring in students is through part-time working. During the term at Manchester, students can work up to 15 hours a week, which more and more are doing for work experience and to cover their loans. If, for instance, you are looking to improve your use of social media or follow up a lead in China, students can give you rapid access to the skills you need at lower cost than you might otherwise expect to pay.

"Students represent a flexible, intelligent workforce," says Milligan, "and graduates give you a fresh pair of eyes, who can see how to improve and change. They all have the ability to think tasks through and are used to working with all sorts of different people."

In considering whether you might approach a university, you do not have to worry about whether it is the beginning or the end of the academic year. "Careers offices are open all year round," says Milligan. "We keep in touch with who is available at any one moment."

18

Graduate recruitment

Looking to grow? Universities can take the strain in finding the right candidate for you

For John Owen, the economics of graduate recruitment are clear. He is the managing director at Goodwin Electronics, a small producer of industrial controls in Liverpool, which has grown 50% in the last two years as manufacturing has recovered.

In adding to his team of 10 specialists to fulfil new orders, he has recently brought in two graduates. "Technically, they have a good mix of skills and can adapt to the changing demands placed on our technology."

His experience of engineers in their late twenties has been less good. "They expect a high salary, but are unlikely to have any direct experience of our sector. We gain more value from taking on graduates at a market rate of £16,000 a year and training them on the job."

He has similar reservations about dealing with recruitment agencies. "They tend to cost a lot and have little knowledge about our type of engineering."

Careers offices have proved more straightforward. "You tell them what you want and they put together a shortlist for you."

In the past, Owen has dealt directly with local universities such as Manchester, Liverpool and Liverpool John Moores, but more recently has worked through Graduate to Merseyside, which is a scheme funded by the EU and meets any costs in recruitment.

He has not experienced any resistance from graduates to the idea of joining an SME. "They like coming to us, because their experience is more varied. It is definitely in our interest to find someone with a fresh outlook, who can make an impact and develop a role in the business."

Contracts are open-ended and Owen expects graduates to stay. His first graduate is only leaving because his girlfriend has moved to Preston, which is too far away to travel to and from every day.

In the last two years, over 250 graduates have taken up similar roles in SMEs through Graduate to Merseyside. Backed by the European Regional Development Fund, the scheme is managed by Steve Wood at the University of Liverpool in collaboration with other higher educators in the region.

"We are not about asking SMEs to do us a favour and give a graduate some experience for six months," says Wood. "Through our networks, we find businesses who want to grow and identify the gaps where they could bring in a graduate.

"We then manage the whole process of agreeing the need, drawing up a spec, screening candidates and drawing up a shortlist. We like to think all the graduates that we put forward could be appointed. It does us no favours if SMEs query the quality of our selection."

Wood draws on graduates from all the universities across Merseyside, as well as those who are returning to the region after finishing their studies elsewhere. Starting salaries are generally between £16,000 and £18,000, depending on the technical skills that a candidate brings to a post.

Appointments have been made across all disciplines and SMEs have found it particularly useful to bring in graduates who can bring their marketing up to speed with social media. "For many SMEs, it is a real struggle to adapt and find new ways of generating opportunities," says Wood, "so graduates can often make an immediate impact."

In the university, Wood gives regular presentations on the advantages and disadvantages of working with SMEs. "You will pick up a lot of responsibility early, working directly with managers and customers. You might be more vulnerable than if you were working for a corporate, but you will never find yourself being a small cog in a big wheel. It is also attractive for those who want to stay in the region once they have graduated."

For now, there is no charge to SMEs for using the scheme and Wood expects to continue in a similar kind of form. "The introduction of tuition fees of £9,000 has re-defined the relationship between universities and their students," he says. "They are going to expect more introductions to potential employers."

19

Sponsoring a researcher

Before diverting resources into running your own research, ask how a university could save you time and money

Yet to start doing your own research? Feel you could add more to what you offer customers? Want to make a mark in your field of knowledge? Maybe even look to explore the boundaries between different disciplines? But are you too short on time to divert resources from day-to-day business and too small to set up your own research programme?

Then as for Emily Humphreys, it might be time to start thinking about sponsoring an up-and-coming researcher at a university. Her company, CRB Discovery, which she has been running with a partner since a buy-out from ICI (Imperial Chemical Industries) in 2000, sits at a point where chemistry crosses into biology.

Her team of 20 graduates from universities such as Durham and Newcastle work as a manufacturing laboratory. As chemists, they synthesise peptides, and as biologists, they create antibodies. Both are tagged and tracked, so medical researchers can explore the mayhem that interactions between proteins in the body can cause.

In pushing the boundaries of peptide chemistry, Humphreys was looking at some new and difficult methods of synthesis. "We have great expertise in the areas in which we are selling, so we could pursue these questions ourselves, if we had the time, but it would distract us from day-to-day business. So it made more sense to find an extra pair of hands who could focus on following through all the implications."

So she turned to the chemistry department at Durham. The project ticked their academic boxes, because it gave them a chance to look at novel compounds and publish their findings. Under the guidance of a professor, who could switch comfortably between chemistry and biology, Humphreys agreed to sponsor a graduate for three years under a CASE fellowship.

She agreed with the university what would be required of the right candidate and met a shortlist of three, before making an appointment. The graduate works at the university, although is due to spend several weeks at CRB. Meetings are held every month to track progress.

So far, Humphreys is really happy with the £7,000 a year she is spending to support the research. She was never expecting any new patents from the work being undertaken, but can see a series of benefits that the collaboration with the university is bringing.

"It allows you to try things out," she says. "At Durham, we get access to analytical equipment and space, which as an SME could never afford to go out and buy."

She also gets an unusually free chance to brainstorm ideas. In business, she finds everyone tends to be cagey. "Academics think differently and talk more openly. Instead of one idea, they will have 10. It is a breath of fresh air."

Humphreys is also finding herself being plugged into wider networks. At the moment, it is mainly by recommendations through the department. Eventually, the results of the research will mean that CRB is cited as a contributor in academic publications. "We might not be doing the research directly, but we can still operate at the forefront of knowledge."

PART 4
Technical advantage

LOUGHBOROUGH UNIVERSITY
SUPPORTING YOUR SUCCESS

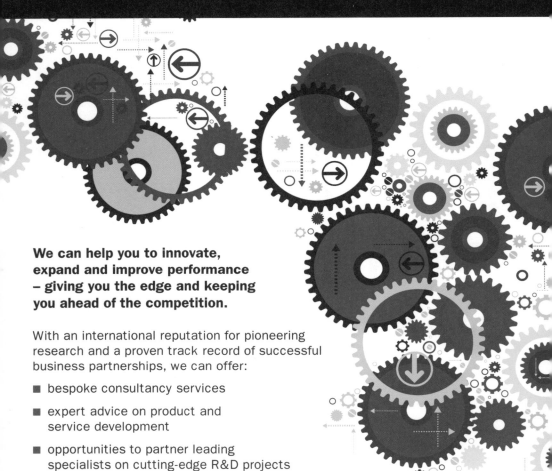

We can help you to innovate, expand and improve performance – giving you the edge and keeping you ahead of the competition.

With an international reputation for pioneering research and a proven track record of successful business partnerships, we can offer:

- bespoke consultancy services
- expert advice on product and service development
- opportunities to partner leading specialists on cutting-edge R&D projects
- secondment opportunities
- high-calibre students keen to gain industry experience during placements
- talented graduates via innovative recruitment programmes
- access to state-of-the-art research facilities
- an outstanding base to grow your business

Contact our Business Development Team:
T. 01509 223110 E. enterprise@lboro.ac.uk
WWW.LBORO.AC.UK/ENTERPRISE

Loughborough University

20

Test models

Use a university's facilities to de-risk your ideas

As an academic entrepreneur, David Park realises the value of being on campus to test his ideas. "As a small company, I don't want to be buying large pieces of capital equipment," he says. "Universities have amazing facilities on which millions have been spent. Pressure is now being applied to make more commercial use of them.

"For us, it means gaining access to kit that we would never be able to buy. Sometimes for free. Sometimes through a third party. Either way, we never have to worry about the overheads."

Originally a research engineer and veteran of two previous spin-outs, Park now specialises in ingredients for food and feed. One flash of insight, on which he then ran numerous tests at the University of Nottingham, is now selling under two licences to Tate & Lyle in a hundred markets around the world.

"Universities are brilliant at the underlying science," he says. "It is not then their job to work out how the results might apply industrially."

Working in the space between the lab and the market, his company, Eminate, spends its time finding ideas with the potential to scale up. The source might be some intellectual property from an academic; it could be some overlooked research from a corporate; or it could be a suggestion from one of his own team of 10.

Since taking over as managing director two years ago, Park has tightened Eminate's commercial focus and moved it to the University of Nottingham's agricultural campus at Sutton Bonington, which covers a full range of disciplines in food and feed, including nutrition, veterinary and biosciences.

The food hall has all the extruders, mixers and driers that anyone might need to check out a new ingredient or recipe. "When resources are so tight, it amazes me so few start-ups use the facilities," says Park. "If you have cooked up a magic sauce and want to test whether it can be manufactured, the university has the expertise to tell you how to scale it up all the way from advising on ingredients to sending out samples."

In producing a pilot, Park is aiming to move well beyond the lab to find out whether he might be able to sell a product in volume. At the same time, he wants to gauge the interest of industrial partners.

At the moment, he is discussing a technique for making us feel full and cutting our blood sugar. Without disclosing any details, he is sounding out whether any of the major players might be interested in a scientifically credible outcome.

Once he is sure of his technical and commercial proof, he can progress to clinical trials, which is when it starts to become expensive. At this point, he might give a first option to one of his industrial partners or ask them to fund the next round of tests.

Park makes use of the university in three other ways to progress his ideas: experts, connections and funds.

1. By being on campus, Park is well placed to build links with leading experts and bring in postgraduates to work on projects. He has just sponsored two doctoral students who have now joined the team.

2. As the MD of an innovative venture, Park might not normally expect to have too much time for networking, yet finds himself being invited to numerous events through the university. "Five minutes with the CTO of a corporate can be invaluable," he says. "It is an intro that money can't buy."

3. By working with the university as a partner, Park has put himself in a position to lead on seven projects supported by the Technology Strategy Board and is applying for a partnership award through a research council which will put up 90% of the funds for some underpinning work. It gives Park the leverage to de-risk ideas that only a multinational might otherwise pursue.

The downside with universities is that the normal rules for managing finances and running projects do not always apply. When academics are working 80 hours a week, your project is unlikely to have top priority. Once you have their attention, costs can mount, delays can happen and results are made public before you are ready. Equally, students will usually have first call on the use of any equipment.

However, universities are under an imperative from policy makers and funding agencies to make a greater impact on business through their research and in their operations. "So you are kicking at an open door," says Park. "If a hundred SMEs wanted to use the food hall at Nottingham in the next year, they would not be turned away."

Park is now testing out his next big idea. If the world's population is going to expand from 7 billion to 9.5 billion in the next 20 years, will we have enough protein to feed everyone? Probably not. So what about insects as a source of protein and unsaturated fat?

"No-one is looking at the commercial potential. Could we find a source of green waste that would not otherwise be used? What protein does a locust or a meal worm have? How healthy or unhealthy are they? Could they be used in the food chain?"

By working with students and technicians, Park is generating some real numbers to drop into his models for production. Externally, his trials would have cost several thousand pounds to run. So far, he has spent a few hundred to check out a market that could be worth millions. "For a small company," argues Park, "there is no better place to be than physically linked to a university that is willing to play."

21

Product design

Want to realise an idea?
Then try building a prototype
through a university

For nearly 40 years, John Pacey Lowrie has been mastering his craft. For those who lose an eye, he makes and paints a replica by hand that fits as closely to reality as possible. His false eyes even respond to the muscle within the socket.

One refinement has always eluded him, however: the dilation of the pupil in response to reduced light. Thirty months ago, he followed up a lead at Nottingham Trent University's centre for smart design. Could it find the technology and the materials to realise his vision at last?

One postgrad and then another took on the challenge as part of their course. At a cost of £4,950 each, Pacey Lowrie now has a prototype that works in principle. Much of the cost was covered by a scheme to support design in local enterprises run by the Future Factory at NTU for the European Regional Development Fund.

Originally, Pacey Lowrie's prototype was the size of a volleyball, but is now more like a tennis ball. It works through a sensor that sends a signal to a carbon paste that sits on an expandable film at the back of the eye.

He has already jointly filed the intellectual property with the university and is intending to sell his technology as a kit under licence for manufacture round the world. As far as Pacey Lowrie can tell, his only competitor clumsily requires users to draw a magnet across their eyes. His innovation is already attracting interest from fellow professionals in the UK, Europe and the US, as well as in India and Africa where a much higher proportion of the population has only eye through lack of medical care.

In the five years since it was founded, NTU's centre for smart design has filed three other patents, as well as a £350,000 grant from the National Institute of Health Research for a technique to re-animate faces after a stroke.

All its work takes its inspiration from finding applications for new technologies and new materials. "As product designers, we are about more than just the aesthetics," says Phil Breedon, reader in smart technologies at NTU. "Our goal is to bridge the gap in the market around developing ideas."

As well as medical devices such as the false eye, the centre specialises in technical textiles, intelligent environments, personal robotics and innovative furniture. Many of its best ideas come when one discipline crosses into another. For instance, its work in wearable devices draws on textiles and robotics, as well as medical devices.

Any enterprise can submit an idea for which it would like a design. At the start of their course, postgraduates will choose which one they would like to pursue.

For them, the chance to work on a live project is a win–win, says Breedon. "They have more to offer potential employers, as well as having their fees paid. So right from the start, they will focus on a project 100%, as well as acquiring all the knowledge to underpin it.

"As a starting point, they will look at what exists at the moment, then review all the materials and technologies that could be used."

So is it a route that Pacey Lowrie would recommend to anyone else? "I would 100% advocate smaller enterprises working with universities," he says, "although you may have to find yourself cracking the whip."

Now that he has a working prototype, he is now making an application through the university for a three-year doctoral student to simplify and miniaturise the technology. "I have been fortunate to work with NTU," says Pacey Lowrie. "Before I made everything by hand in wax and plastic, so knew nothing about how smart materials might be used. Now we are close to being able to give the impression that a pupil in a false eye is dilating as normal."

22

Production upgrades

Make a technology leap to capture future growth

A conversation with representitives of a university at an exhibition in 2010 is about to result in a new line of manufacturing technology in Sheffield. For 40 years, William Beckett Plastics has specialised in packaging for cutting tools, exporting 80% of its annual sales of £4m. It is a high-volume, low-cost business, in which Beckett has excelled, winning two Queen's awards for export.

So what scope might they now have for extending their expertise to an emerging area of demand that lies outside their current field of operation? In aerospace and medical equipment, the company could sense that interest was rising in the moulding of metal alloys. As well as being lower in weight, carbon and waste, such parts could be designed in complex and intricate geometries that designers might otherwise have thought too ambitious.

Unlike plastics, injection moulding of metal alloys is a high-quality, low-run business, which depends heavily on innovation in powdered materials. At the University of Sheffield, the Mercury Centre has been created to map out the potential uses to which metals, ceramics and polymers can be put in designing and producing complex parts that require no further finishing on delivery.

In transferring this knowledge into use at Beckett, Lukas Jirinek was chosen as the research associate. Originally a graduate in polymers in the Czech Republic, he had worked in metal injection moulding at one of Germany's Frauenhof centres for technology and innovation.

Employed by the university within a Knowledge Transfer Partnership (KTP), he started on site at Beckett in January 2011. Two-thirds of his costs were met by the Technology Strategy Board. The rest was covered by the company.

His challenge was to take what worked in the lab into full-scale production. Few small manufacturers are likely to have the analytical tools to generate the data required by major buyers in aerospace or medical equipment. His advantage was that he could continue to work under the supervision of the university, as well as drawing on all its equipment and resources.

The Mercury Centre is a £12m facility, part funded by the EU, which has a state-of-the-art factory floor and a wide array of analytical equipment. Within its mission, it is expressly seeking to give companies in the region around Sheffield an insight into future manufacturing technologies and speed up the rate at which they are adopted.

"For an SME who wants to make a technology leap and potentially find a new recruit, KTPs are about the best tool they can use," says Neale Daniel, Sheffield Engineering Gateway Manager. "The university will recruit the candidate for you, so you don't have to worry about the HR. You will end up with a top-ranking graduate for only £30,000 a year whose progress will be measured against a series of milestones set by the university."

At the end of his two-year programme, Jirinek was appointed technical manager of a new spin-out company, Beckett MIM (metal injection moulding). Based on his work during his KTP, the company has won a £1m package backed by the Regional Growth Fund to build a separate production facility in Sheffield.

Currently, it is the only capability of its kind in the UK. As well as steels, it can mass-produce designs in other metals such as titanium, tungsten, nickel and copper, as well as different alloys, that might otherwise be impossible to machine.

The other advantage of a KTP is that it can create a strong foundation for a continuing relationship with the university. The Mercury Centre has already introduced Beckett to one of its first customers for metal injection moulding and has inspired a patent for a technical fixer that can be produced without any form of cutting, as well as being 20% lighter than any of its rivals.

From January 2013, a second engineer was recruited from the university and another KTP is underway. This time, the objective is to explore what other alloys could be deployed by designers in aerospace and medical equipment,

"For Beckett, it has been a move into a completely new business," says Jirinek. "Our hope now is that we can start to grow rapidly."

As he points out, the composition of tungsten alloys has barely changed in the last 60 years. Through the manufacturing techniques it is adopting, Beckett is putting itself in a position to offer more flexibility and creativity in how materials are used for complex designs in future.

23

Buy in ideas

Even if you are small, you can change the game and escape price pressures by bringing in new science

What do you do if you have been in business since 1786 but can hear the approaching tread of low-cost Chinese competitors? For Peter Wilkes at Vale Brothers in Walsall who make saddles, horse rugs and stable equipment under royal warrant, the answer came from somewhere completely unexpected. The bathroom.

In 2010, he was having an exploratory discussion with Coventry University. What could he do to control the spread of the bacteria and funguses that every horse owner dreads?

Strangles, in particular, is a respiratory condition which is usually enough to end a horse's career. It might be relatively rare, but its effects can be devastating. One race track in the US was forced to close for six weeks. More common are fungal infections, such as ringworm, to which horses fall regularly prone.

A similar affliction, although in a completely different environment, was being investigated by microbiologists at Coventry University: the black mould that grows between the tiles in the bathroom. They were adapting a technique pioneered in the US to remove cellular organisms without using chemicals. Instead, a tiny spike on the surface pierced and killed them.

As a side effect, the cells were electrocuted as well. The nitrogen used in the additive for the spike produced a positive charge. When combined with the negative one in the membrane of the cell, it was blown to smithereens, thereby bringing the shine back to a bathroom.

This technique offered two advantages over chemicals. First, cells could build up no resistance to being spiked. Second, product approvals were easier and faster to gain.

But would it work in the stables? What would happen if you put these spikes on the plastic bristles of a brush? Through the university, Wilkes conducted a series of tests on the strangles bacteria and the ringworm fungus. After a couple of months, it was found that 99.9% of all cells were dead within 24 hours.

For any groom in a stable yard, Wilkes knew that was too long to wait. All of the horses could be infected by then. So he commissioned another set of tests to investigate the clear-up within eight minutes, which was the least amount of time that the science would allow. The results were the same.

Wilkes now knew he had a product that he could take to market. If he could save horse owners the cost of treatments and dispel the fear of the spread of infection, he felt confident that he could push the price of a typical brush at retail from an existing £3.95 to £13.95. "Why wouldn't you?" he says. "In our industry, it changes the game."

At the moment, Vale Brothers, which Wilkes bought out in 1999, turns over £3.5m a year. On the new anti-bacterial and anti-fungal range, he estimates he can sell an extra £1.5m a year under the brand KBF99 (kills bacteria and fungus 99%).

So far, he has spent £20,000 on tests in the microbiology labs at Coventry University and he is about to verify whether his new technique is equally effective against two of the other most common complaints from which horses suffer: mud fever and rain scald.

On the commercial side, Coventry University is taking out worldwide patents on the use of these spikes in the equine market. Vale Brothers will operate under an exclusive licence. As well as sharing in some of the costs for this intellectual property, it will be paying the university a royalty on sales.

The first target for Wilkes is the 900,000 horses in the UK. So far, the reaction from users has been encouragingly positive. However, the trade is reluctant to make any forward orders in current economic conditions, so the launch will be slower than Wilkes might like.

"We have enough stockists already. Everyone else will have to place a forward order. We cannot afford to take a risk on a long production run."

Realistically, he is not expecting anyone to order the full range of 24 brushes, buckets and other pieces of stable equipment, which will retail for a total of £220. It is much more likely that orders for four or five items will be made, which will then build up gradually.

In Europe, he is working through his existing distributors and an initial order is expected from the US. Worldwide there are a total of 60 million horses. Many are still a working part of everyday life, particularly in the new economic powers like China and Brazil, and Wilkes is hoping that his brushes will start to open up these markets.

The KBF99 range was launched to the equine industry in early 2012. Such events are relatively informal in Wilkes's experience. This time, he had invited the microbiologists from Coventry to give their account of how the science worked. "It might have been detailed, but it showed how serious we are and how big our products could be," says Wilkes.

What advice would he give anyone else who was thinking about working with a university? "It is simpler than you expect," he says. "You only pay for the expert as long as you are using them, even if it is just for a month or two.

"The scientists also tend to bring in their colleagues on particular issues. At some points, we had three or four leading experts in the field working on our innovation.

"The gains you make can be significant," says Wilkes. "It is always better to work as a team than on your own. We will definitely be bringing more science into the business and we are already looking at our next project with Coventry."

LIVERPOOL JOHN MOORES UNIVERSITY

Impact through
Research, Collaboration and **Innovation.**

Find out how LJMU could work with your organisation

LJMU Research and Innovation Services

t. 0500 876543

e. bdc@ljmu.ac.uk

www.ljmu.ac.uk/businessengagement

dream plan **achieve**

24

Research on demand

Set academics a challenge and you can find some creative – and lucrative – answers

Whether in aerospace or life sciences, Ward Hills has been throwing problems at universities for the last 15 years. He has yet to be disappointed, even though his model for innovation might strike some as unusual.

First, he spots the potential for a software product and describes how it is going to be different. Only then does he ask universities such as Cambridge, Imperial, Loughborough, Southampton or UCL to make it happen technologically.

All told, he has placed 10 short-term contracts to run a study or write some software. "As long as I have asked a good question, I have never had a bad answer," he says.

His latest venture, Pneumacare, sprang from the frustration that a doctor felt in measuring the breath of vulnerable children at Addenbrooke's Hospital in Cambridge. If he wanted to know how the lungs of a newborn were working, he felt that current procedures were too invasive and results were too slow in arriving.

Together the doctor and Hills put their minds to finding an alternative. They deliberately steered clear of looking at existing technologies and focused on the features that a new product should have.

"We wanted to be kinder and gentler for patients, as well as more informative for doctors," says Hills, 45, who did his own postgraduate studies in remote sensors at Washington State University, before leaving the US 20 years ago to pursue a career in the technology business.

At the end of his original spec for a new way of measuring how someone's lungs were performing, he deliberately left an empty black box into which a technology could be dropped, whatever it might be. He then went to speak to the research director at Cambridge University to ask for suggestions on which of his colleagues might be able to help.

In response to a circular on email, Joan Lazenby, a lecturer in engineering, thought her technique for capturing the motion of dancers and athletes in 3D could be translated into a solution. In fact, patients were likely to be easier to track, because they were lying still.

In a couple of weeks, she had rigged up a working prototype from gear that she already had lying about the laboratory. Essentially, she used two cameras to project a 3D image of the chest in a way that could capture data on how someone was breathing.

Even at this stage, the medical potential in 3D graphics originally developed for entertainment was clear. Instead of being forced to take deep breaths, patients could be measured as they slept or were under anaesthesia. Doctors could back up their judgements with a set of figures which they could act on immediately, leave for colleagues later or send for a second opinion.

It represented a complete change in diagnostics, says Hills, who in principle could see one of his devices being fitted to every bed in intensive care in the UK, then Europe and the US.

To start developing these ideas, Hills found two small grants and signed up Lazenby on a short-term research contract. Within a year, she had written the algorithms and developed the hardware to fill the black box at the end of the original spec.

Hills now had a prototype that he could put in front of doctors. In observing how it was used, he set up a three-way collaboration between the university, the hospital and the business. He wanted to make sure that the academics clearly understood the medical and commercial reasons for developing any particular function. In this way, he was able to shorten the design process and save himself two to three years.

The other advantage of giving Lazenby's engineers access to data from the hospital was that they could make suggestions that the doctors had not considered themselves. In particular, the researchers saw the scope for using 3D graphics to spot more conditions. Were the chest and the belly moving in sync when patients were breathing? Was the right side of the chest moving faster than the left side? These patterns could provide a fast and non-intrusive way of catching and tracking conditions such as asthma, bronchitis and emphysema.

Pointers from Ward Hills on research contracts

- Put specific requests for technology to the university.

- Set expectations and ground rules early.

- Be clear about what is happening and maintain close relationships with everyone.

- Shorten time in development by putting the university close to the customer.

- Work out the motivation for academics in pursuing research.

- Define a project by July, if you want a graduate to start work for the next academic year.

A specialist designer started to prepare the product for market, although the university remains as Pneumacare's "deep research wing". Lazenby works on a straight consultancy contract and Pneumacare funds at least one graduate a year. Under a pipeline agreement it has first refusal on work in specific areas.

All the medical IP is held by Pneumacare under a patent. Lazenby and her colleagues, however, have shares in the company, so will have a stake in its future success.

One of Lazenby's graduates is now Pneumacare's director of software and still spends one day a week in the engineering department to make refinements and build new capabilities.

The commercial office of the university, Cambridge Enterprise, has played the role of a supportive facilitator and has invested in the company, as well as taking a seat on the board. All told, £2.4m has been raised in three rounds to bring Pneumacare to market.

It launched in the UK in July 2011, three years after the idea was first discussed, and is now being introduced to the US as well. The model for measuring the intensity of someone's breathing sells for £15,000 and the more sophisticated diagnostic version for £25,000. If all goes well and the challenge of educating medical users can be met, Hills estimates that sales could be in the tens of thousands.

So what advice would he have for anyone else who is setting up a similar relationship with a university? "It can be a real problem in combining the academic and commercial mindsets. Everyone has to be clear about what is happening.

"You have to maintain all the relationships, so no-one feels that they are being taken advantage of. If cash is all going in one direction and the research in another, arrangements can feel asymmetric. You have to set expectations and ground rules early.

"Everyone has to understand timescales. Ventures can run out of cash, so six weeks can be a matter of survival. Universities like to fit into the nine months of the academic year, so graduate students have to be in place by July.

"You also have to work out the currencies in which everyone is dealing. Younger academics will be looking to publish papers and improve their prospects of becoming a professor. Older academics might be looking for funds to build research teams. Corporations may be looking to position themselves in a particular way.

"Sometimes the solutions from the university are not practical or economic. Usually, you will find something worth discussing commercially. Every once in a while, you will find a jewel."

25

Research clusters

Shared platforms are opening up knowledge and speeding up routes to market

When a new market is hurtling towards you, you are unlikely to have much time to craft your own answer in the lab. Instead, you might turn to one of the shared platforms for innovation that many universities are now developing.

These are designed to bring together all those in the chain of creating innovation, so they can test out new techniques and explore different ways of making a commercial return. The principle is that the best ideas are usually found at the interface between different roles, so a free flow of knowledge and insights is encouraged.

For industries such as the life sciences, it represents a radical transformation. "The fully integrated R&D model is out of date and has to be reinvented to turn fledgling ideas into life-changing medicines," comments David Docherty at the new National Centre for Universities and Business. "Pharma companies are increasingly embracing open innovation, outsourcing their R&D, working with young biotech companies, and gathering themselves into basic research clusters with universities, improving their access to academic talent and their ability to tap into small innovative firms."

The goal for companies such as GSK is to create "powerhouses of problem solving", says Docherty: "to achieve that, the boundaries between academia, the NHS, research institutes, and their supply and value chain have to become more porous".

The objective of such clusters, whether in biomedicines or in other challenges such as clean energy, future cities or cyber security, is to co-create growth by pooling resources and sharing the risks. Usually located around a university, the entire ecosystem of innovation can come together, creating a point around which knowledge, talent and funding can interact. The hope, according to Professor Birgitte Andersen at the Big Innovation Centre, is that they can develop "the convening power" to become anchor institutions.

A research factory in Bristol is starting to realise the potential for finding new applications in composites in this way. Two years ago, leading manufacturers combined with the university to launch a national centre for excellence, which was built over 17,000 square metres at a cost of £60m.

For Rolls-Royce, GKN and Airbus, the use of carbon fibre in particular could have far-reaching implications for their future designs. They may not make it themselves, but they want a proper understanding of how the technology might evolve.

Operating as a subsidiary of the university, the National Composites Centre has as its focus the building of capability to take new knowledge into the market. It occupies the point halfway between research and industry, often known as the "valley of death" as it has so often witnessed the demise of promising technologies in the past.

At one end of its operation, the NCC develops early-stage ideas for possible adoption by industrial users. At the other, it runs collaborative programmes with leading players and their supply chains to resolve challenges in engineering.

In working on such projects, the attitude of a Tier One supplier such as Rolls-Royce is that it will continue to protect its exclusivity in scoping out future products over the next 20 years. However, in making the kinds of process improvements over the two to three years in which the NCC specialises, its ethos is that it will share its knowledge freely with its partners.

As well as making technical improvements, the NCC pursues "an aggressive development of skills" within the supply chain. No-one wants to repeat the mistakes of the past when new technologies underperformed because of a lack of capability in their use.

Smaller companies in the supply chain can join the NCC as Tier Two members for £30,000 a year, which gives them the right to make use of equipment and set up projects. Just as significantly, they get the chance to get close to strategic partners and Tier One customers in working on collaborative projects.

The next phase of development for the NCC, which is now underway, is to build a series of cells to accommodate SMEs on site. Ultimately, the goal is to create a full campus for composites on the science park at Bristol.

Clusters such as these have the potential to join up all the pieces within an innovation, which if pursued in isolation, might not otherwise have happened. For the leading players, it speeds up how they identify and deploy ideas. For universities, it creates an active market for technology on their doorstep. For smaller companies in the supply chain, it opens up new sources of knowledge and capital. For everyone, it can lead to the creation of new ventures and new intellectual property.

26

Research partnerships

In all areas of knowledge, programmes are being run to connect universities to business

Britain is a major player in research and consistently attracts a disproportionate share of international projects. These activities are not conducted in isolation.

Each of the UK's seven research councils pursue their activities in close partnership with business. First, because they want to make sure that they are addressing challenges in the real world, and, second, they are looking to ensure that any research ultimately has an economic and social impact.

The seven UK research councils

1. Arts & Humanities Research Council (AHRC)

2. Biotechnology & Biological Sciences Research Council (BBSRC)

3. Economic & Social Research Council (ESRC)

4. Engineering & Physical Sciences Research Council (EPSRC)

5. Medical Research Council (MRC)

6. Natural Environment Research Council (NERC)

7. Science & Technology Facilities Council (STFC)

Under the strategic lead of Research Councils UK (RCUK), a total of £3bn in funding is awarded every year to universities, covering the complete spectrum of knowledge.

"We encourage a two-way flow of knowledge and expertise to ensure our world-leading research continues to contribute to the economic growth and wellbeing of the nation," says Alexandra Saxon at RCUK. "As well as programmes and facilities, we invest in a flow of people between universities and business at every stage of their careers."

All told, the research councils are directly engaged with 2,500 companies and over a fifth of all postgraduates studying for their doctorates have a formal link to business as part of their research. At each stage of the process of creating and applying new knowledge, smaller companies can become involved in the work of the research councils.

Directions

On each of the research councils, representatives from large and small companies are involved in reviewing proposals and giving strategic advice. In-depth groups also work to align the development of postgraduate skills with future demands from business.

Outlets

To improve the chances of turning knowledge into growth and finding new applications, research councils run different outlets to let collaboration happen. The Engineering & Physical Sciences Research Council (EPSRC), for instance, has set up 12 centres for innovative manufacturing at universities across the UK. At each one, research is undertaken into challenges and opportunities, supported by leading industry partners and high-tech enterprises.

Such transfers happen beyond science as well. In the creative economy, the Arts & Humanities Research Council (AHRC) supports hubs, where smaller companies can develop ideas, consult experts and use state-of-the-art digital equipment.

Awards

Through the research councils, awards are made for bringing in high-level skills and opening up research. These collaborative grants for training, known as CASE studentships, support postgraduates in resolving a business challenge in pursuit of their doctorate. They are expected to work within both a commercial and an academic framework, spending a significant proportion of their time within the business.

Secondments

In resolving challenges and making innovations, a more immediate way of encouraging flows of people between universities and companies is through secondments. Research councils run flexible schemes to set them up without too much hassle. Over 100 have taken place in the last two years, mainly to smaller companies.

Other ways of setting up temporary switches from and into universities are available. The Biotechnology and Biological Sciences Research Council (BBSRC) runs internships for PhD students, which it sees as vital in preparing them for their future careers.

Markets

To speed up the time it takes for innovation to reach the market, research councils take a role in incubating research outcomes and supporting mechanisms for supporting knowledge. Each has a team to advise on intellectual property, spin-outs and commercial transfers.

For example, the Science & Technology Facilities Council (STFC) has an office for technology transfer, which manages the rights in any intellectual property that is created through its programmes. The technology arm of the Medical Research Council (MRC) plays a similar role. In 2010/11, it generated £65.8m in income from licensing from discoveries and invention through the MRC.

Campuses

To turn innovation into growth, research councils back a number of campuses to open up world-class facilities and infrastructure to business. On the research and innovation campus at Babraham, one of six sites run by the BBSRC, experts in bioscience are located next to biotech entrepreneurs, so increasing the chances for crossovers between theory and practice.

Similarly, the STFC is a major partner on two leading campuses, Daresbury and Harwell. Both became enterprise zones last year, which means lower taxes and easier planning for enterprises.

In each case, the objective is to create a vibrant community of technology ventures. At somewhere like Harwell, the results are clear. Over 4,500 people work there employed in a hundred different enterprises.

For more information about Research Councils UK, visit www.rcuk.ac.uk

PART 5
Business advantage

working with you...

...funded support for small and medium businesses

At Nottingham Trent University we work with businesses in all sectors. Our **working with you** project offers small and medium businesses access to our expertise, services and facilities.

Our dedicated account managers interpret business needs and provide one-to-one support. As well as specialist workshops and academic consultancy we focus on helping businesses to develop and improve.

Talent

We can help with short or long-term placements or permanent staff recruitment.

Skills

The right support can increase business confidence leading to innovation, opportunity and increased productivity.

Innovation

From product design to effective marketing, our experts can drive innovation that makes a real difference to your business.

To find out more and register for updates, please contact us.

Tel: +44 (0)115 848 8899

Email: workingwithyou@ntu.ac.uk

www.ntu.ac.uk/workingwithyou

Project Part-Financed by the European Union

European Regional Development Fund

NOTTINGHAM TRENT UNIVERSITY

27

The growth plan

Do you have a vision? Then a university might be the best place to crystallise it

Jerome Baddley was facing one of the classic dilemmas for anyone trying to grow an organisation. He had recently become one of the first to measure a carbon footprint for an NHS trust. As a result of his review, emissions were down 25%; a performance that won him and his colleagues at the Nottingham Energy Partnership a global award for sustainability from the *British Medical Journal* in 2011.

You would have thought it was a perfect platform for building their work with eight large public bodies in the East Midlands. The trouble, as many small practices have experienced, is that you are then either intensely busy or you have a quiet patch until the next job starts.

So Baddley and his fellow senior managers took the decision to reduce the variability of their work and to start engaging more with smaller companies in the East Midlands. Externally, it made sense, because large contractors wanted their suppliers to reduce their carbon risks.

Internally, it reinforced the overall mission at the Nottingham Energy Partnership, which had started as a charity in 1997 to cut fuel poverty, before expanding into a social enterprise to find efficiencies in the use of energy domestically and commercially. Since 2008, turnover in this business has grown fast and is now up to £4m a year. Any profits are recycled back into the charity.

But how could Baddley and his colleagues realise their vision for cleaning up the local supply chain? Their answer was to turn to their local university, Nottingham Trent.

"We have collaborated with each other on a number of different levels," says Baddley. "For us, it has proved highly productive in reaching our market and developing our service."

His first point of contact was at the business school. Decisions about the direction of the business might have been taken, but no-one had drawn them together into a formal plan.

"It is difficult in any busy organisation to write a strategy," comments Baddley. "It really helps if someone external can help you to think creatively and structure the thoughts which you have already had. It was at the university that we found the space and inspiration to develop."

As a result of this process, NEP now has a clear model to offer smaller companies: switch, save, generate and share. Save costs by switching to the right deal. Find all possible efficiencies. Take the chance to generate your own power. Share your performance by gaining a standard.

As the final piece in its strategic design, NEP has adopted a template for environmental management by taking on the franchise in Nottingham and Derby for Investors in the Environment. However, for Baddley, the question still remained as to how he could create a compelling offer for local SMEs. This time, he turned to the Future Factory, an EU funded programme for sustainable design at NTU.

Normally, an SME could expect to pay £2,000 for an environmental management system. Through Investors in the Environment, the cost might drop to £1,500. By working with the Future Factory, NEP has found a model that it can offer at £350.

By drawing on some EU funding, it is able to train and recruit students as environmental consultants as part of their course. Under NEP's supervision, they take companies through all the preliminary steps, before Baddley and his team of 18 consultants become directly involved in making a final submission for accreditation by the Investors in the Environment.

Launched the previous October, 15 assignments had been completed by Easter 2014. In the future, Baddley is expecting many more of the 120 students in environmental science at NTU to become involved.

His next project at the university is to start teaching environmental management at the business school, both to current students and to managers within larger organisations. For him, it reflects a genuine willingness by the university to engage.

"NTU is outward facing in everything it does and is open to working in real partnership. You might think it might want to keep any European funding to pay its own staff. Instead, it has sought different ways to support us in reaching our market."

28

IT solutions

Cut the cost of bringing your software up to date by giving a student an opportunity to learn

For any enterprise looking for growth, it makes sense to go online. In Britain, the web economy now accounts for 8.5% of all activity, higher than any of the world's other leading markets. It is a figure that is likely to keep spiralling up to judge by the experience of online groceries, which already account for 5% of the retail market and are growing at 15% a year.

As a small business, it can be hard to join the action. You are unlikely to be able to stretch to your own IT operation. Alternatively, even if you can afford the cost of bringing in an IT consultant, the solutions tend to be more sophisticated than you need and would soon have to be updated.

In Kent, a solution is being developed for the 70% of companies in the county whose turnover is less than £250,000 a year. An IT clinic (KITC) has been created for them in the university's school of computing which has the aim of bringing them up to speed on how to apply the latest techniques in managing their software, telecoms, databases, websites and networks.

Any implementation is deliberately kept simple. On each project, the goal is to design a solution which can easily be maintained and which will last as the business grows.

The formula for making this support possible is that student consultants work on the IT challenges that any enterprise might be facing. For them, it is treated as a learning opportunity, rather than a paid assignment, so making it possible for all kinds of business to access their expertise.

Student consultants

Any consultancy is generally performed by those in the final year of their studies in computer science. Their work is supervised by a full-time manager, Jason Marshall, who manages the clinic's day-to-day operations and implements its strategy. This work is supervised by an advisory board comprising senior figures in education and business whose role is set the right course for the clinic, its students and its users.

The students' work is assessed against a matrix of six academic outcomes, which cover the key consultancy skills that they will develop in the course of their assignments. They demonstrate their capability in these skills by writing reflective reports, analysing both the things that have gone well, and reflecting on areas for improvement, both for themselves and for the organisation.

Technology outcomes

For a small company, it can be hard to ask IT consultants the right questions, says the manager of KITC, Jason Marshall.

> "Any challenges you are experiencing within the business often appear to be unique. The usual response from an IT perspective is to custom-build a fully bespoke software solution that exactly resolves the difficulties you are currently facing.
>
> "However, the elegant design for today's problem rarely stands still. The problem with such bespoke solutions is that the problem domain that they are designed to solve rarely remains static. Instead, over time the domain shifts as the business itself develops requiring the solution to evolve to meet this change.
>
> "At the KITC, we believe any IT solution should be sustainable. Users will want to keep using it because it continues to work, not because they are locked into any particular product."

So what is the best approach for smaller companies in Kent to take when working with their student consultants? Marshall recommends a three-stage approach.

1. **Technology foundation:** most IT problems are at some level shared between many businesses. Where these common problem domains have been identified, broad application frameworks exist that help to solve these problems. By helping our customers to see their problems in the wider context, and identifying the general problem domain, we can then help them to see how these standard frameworks can work to solve their individual problems.

2. **Technology guidance:** the next stage is to understand how the customer's exacting requirements can be met using these frameworks by analysing the customer's requirements and provide guidance as to which framework will provide the best fit.

3. **Implementation:** the final stage is to provide an implementation service that implements the technology, configures it for the customer's needs, and then trains the customer so that they are able to use and maintain the system without further assistance.

Right skills

For the students, two challenges can face them when they leave and start to look for work. Do they have the "soft" skills required to work in teams and manage projects? And do they have the applied technical skills for which employers are looking?

"The IT sector is now so broad and heterogeneous that it would be impossible to train graduates to any significant depth in all of the technologies that they could be exposed to in their career," argues Marshall. "Instead courses often concentrate on a small number of core concepts, embodied in a selection of technologies, whilst giving graduates the ability to learn other technologies for themselves as required. However what traditional courses fail to do is adequately prepare students to apply these skills and technical know-how to real world situations."

His aim is that with the experience of working with an SME through the KITC, students can develop both their soft and technical skills.

> "By focusing on consultancy for small businesses, the students are able to develop their communication skills, in particular those that allow them to deal more effectively with clients. Furthermore, all of the work that they carry out is to solve real

business problems. The students quickly learn to use professional empathy to understand the problem from the business perspective, and then to collaborate with their colleagues to develop a sustainable solution to that problem, often requiring them to pick up new skills and technologies. "

29

Marketing strategy and process

A university can ask the awkward questions to set your marketing on the right course

For years, Carl Harris had been selling into a market in which business walked through the door. In 2010, he could see this happy scenario was about to change.

The business which he had founded in Bradford in 1990, Universal AV, had been selling audiovisual equipment to universities and schools: the projectors, the screens and the sound equipment, as well as the controls for bringing everything together into presentations that students would find hard to forget.

Such business is no longer there for the taking. "Up until then we had not really had a marketing strategy," says Harris. "To move forward, we were going to have to learn more about our customers and why they liked dealing with us."

At the same time as cuts were happening in the public sector, Harris was running a commercial service for organisers of events for corporations such as Rio Tinto. Orders were holding up well for someone who could run the technical side of a show or presentation.

When Harris first met Martin Haley, a lecturer in marketing at the University of Bradford, he was wondering about the scope of integrating his two brands to create some crossover. During their initial discussions, it became clear that more fundamental questions were being raised.

"We were going to have to change our shoes and start thinking like our customers," says Harris. "We already had a sense of where our strengths lay, but the university gave us a broader perspective and raised some awkward questions about what we were doing. We realised that marketing was not something that could just happen on its own."

On the back of these conversations, Harris agreed an 18-month collaboration with Haley and the management school to review Universal AV's marketing strategy. Under this Knowledge Transfer Partnership, he selected a research associate, Alex Beardsley, from among a number of candidates.

Supervised by Haley, she spent six months understanding the position in which Universal AV found itself and where it wanted to go; in the following six months she drew up a strategy; and in her final six months she put in place the marketing tools that Universal AV could then start using.

Universal AV's logo and website have been re-designed. A book of brand rules has been put in place. Social media is being used to trail Universal AV's strengths in 3D projection and augmented reality. A marketing department has been created.

"We have been on a tremendous learning curve," says Harris. "We have a much better understanding of our customers and what we bring to them."

For him, the £28,000 cost of the KTP has been money well spent. "It has given us a lasting legacy. We could have brought in a marketing consultant who would have produced a glossy brochure for us. But we would not have understood what had to happen next."

After the KTP finished in 2011, Universal AV continued to do well in a difficult market. Turnover rose to £10m and sales in education moved well ahead of target. Harris even found himself in a position to buy the assets of an events company that ran into trouble. As well as offices in Bradford and Newcastle, he now has operations in Manchester, Cardiff and Rugby, taking his total headcount up to 68.

For Haley, the project with Universal AV is a lesson in the power of clarity and consistency. "You want to give a positive image and create a strong predisposition to buy from you. But in re-discovering what their business is about, companies tend to look at the skills they have developed rather than how the market is evolving."

In his experience, the danger when you grow is that sub-brands are created unintentionally. "You want to focus on supporting just one in the right marketplace. Any changes are likely to confuse your customers. They don't like change. They want to know what you stand for.

"So never confuse marketing with promotions," he says. "Marketing starts with a plain piece of paper and a search for what customers actually expect from you. Once you create a match with an understanding of how you operate, you can avert the danger of straying into areas where you are less strong."

Do you know?

The University of Hertfordshire is the UK's leading business-facing university.

Offering a diverse range of business services, we put ourselves at the forefront striving to shape, support and grow your business with our expertise and state of the art facilities.

Our wealth of academic expertise, talented students and postgraduates are able to support your business needs in:

- **Research and Development** for new technologies and products
- **Knowledge Transfer** with access to University talent and know-how
- **Consultancy** across many industries including: engineering and business

- **Innovation Vouchers** for small business and the voluntary sector
- **Market Research Service** delivering professional support across life sciences sectors
- **Sustainable business development** showcasing resource efficient practice

Contact us to find out more:

+ 44 (0) 1707 286406   be@herts.ac.uk   www.herts.ac.uk/businessservices

30

Management development programmes

For small business owners, it can be surprisingly tough to take decisions on moving forward and up

Grow your business from £250,000 to a couple of million? Take your headcount from four to 20? Phil Taylor is giving it a go.

After 10 years in software, he has bought into an existing enterprise in Skelmersdale. One of the two founding directors had decided to retire and Taylor saw the potential for growth at IT Managed, which runs IT on contract for smaller companies in the north-west of England.

"We offer a must-have service at a fixed cost. Enterprises just pay a quarterly fee. With us, they can forget any worries about employing someone or running up extras."

Up until Taylor arrived, the business had grown slowly by word of mouth. "We were just a few techies without any sales or marketing."

In drawing up his plans, he was talking to an adviser from a local agency for business support about training for his staff. "What about you?", she asked him. As a business owner in his early 50s, Taylor remembers being vaguely insulted. He had always thought management education was too formal or too corporate for someone like him.

His adviser pointed him towards LEAD, a programme run through a number of universities in the north-west of England. Putting aside his reservations, he went to an open day at Liverpool University. He liked it immediately.

Taylor saw the chance to pick up a set of techniques about which he suddenly realised he knew less than he thought. "It seemed practical common sense," he says. "It is a course for everyone. You don't need any particular qualifications or intelligence."

Designed for those who run a business with fewer than 50 employees, the course has been running since 2004. Over the course of 10 months, participants focus on two main challenges: how to grow their business and how to develop their own skills as leaders.

"It is not easy for a small business owner to take a step back and look at the bigger picture," says Richard Holloway, who organises the LEAD courses at Liverpool University. "Daily pressures decide the priorities."

Leadership can make a big difference, he says. "It's about the ability to make tough decisions, to seek out new opportunities and capitalise on the skills of your staff."

For Phil Taylor, it cured one of the headaches that most SME owners experience: how to manage people. "I have always had a feel for emotional intelligence, but had no terms in which to express it," he says. "For me, it was suddenly 'wow', when one of our first lectures explained how it works.

"It lets you play to an employee's strengths and understand their weaknesses. You are better placed to make sure everyone is engaged and spot any trouble before it happens."

The course took up a couple of days of Taylor's time each month. In structure, it was split between coaching in particular skills and discussions between participants about real challenges within each other's businesses. It was a supportive experience that Taylor really enjoyed.

"Instead of someone saying, 'you should do this', I was asked 'have you thought about this?' In building your confidence, it makes a huge difference."

Taylor has taken away a number of other techniques. In finance, his forecasts for cashflow and his understanding of business ratios have improved. In innovation, he is developing more new offerings and finding ways to make them different.

He has also gained a clear understanding of the distinction between management and leadership. "Managers will take you from A to B. Leaders create a path that can take you much further."

Normally, the course costs between £7,000 and £8,000, although Taylor received two grants, so only paid £1,000. Like many SMEs, the full expense might have put him off initially, although he is relieved he was given the chance to take part.

"LEAD has enhanced my enthusiasm and fired me up. It is probably the best thing I have done in my career."

Although the course has finished, he and the rest of his LEAD group now organise presentations themselves and meet regularly to review challenges within their businesses. In addition, Taylor has just enrolled for a master's in management at Edge Hill University and is then hoping to qualify as a chartered director.

And his business? In the two years after he bought into it, turnover doubled to £600,000 and five more people joined. "We are getting into a good position to springboard our growth and aim for £2m and beyond."

LEAD was developed and piloted by Lancaster University Management School in conjunction with the Northwest Regional Development Agency. As well as Liverpool and Lancaster, it is run through the following universities: Manchester Metropolitan, Central Lancashire, Cumbria and Salford.

PART 6
Appendices

Appendix 1
Innovation vouchers

Many universities use "innovation vouchers" as a way of engaging SMEs for the first time. Since September 2012, the Technology Strategy Board (TSB) has taken up the running with a national scheme. Devolved authorities in Scotland, Wales and Northern Ireland all run their own versions.

Broadly, they all display similar characteristics. As a smaller company, you receive £3,000–£5,000 to conduct an initial project in pursuit of an innovation with a knowledge specialist, who will typically be an expert at a university or at a research institute, but could be an IP adviser, a technical consultant or a designer. You might want to explore a new idea for a project. Or it could be a question of how you manage the process of bringing an innovation to the market. Either way you can only use innovation vouchers once, although they can often lead follow-up sources of funding.

Pete Higgins at UWI Technology is one entrepreneur who has benefited. He used his £5,000 with Heriot-Watt to fund his search for a technique to give an accurate alert for when to use food or medicine once you have opened it. It was a productive exercise. UWI has pulled in nearly £200,000 in funding and Higgins is pursuing a licensing strategy for smart labels with the aim of making £8m in profit within five years.

Newcastle is one university that has run its own scheme for innovation vouchers, which has resulted in 125 new engagements with SMEs, and Aston co-ordinates 13 universities in the West Midlands which have so far run 670 projects.

Eligibility will be similar to Glasgow's First Step Awards, which are designed to "create long-term collaborations between small companies and the university, especially new partnerships. Priority will be given to projects that assess both the potential and feasibility of a new product, process or market and can lead to opportunities to attract follow-on funding from existing sources, demonstrate a clear route to market or indicate a step change in current processes within a micro or small enterprise."

Nationally, the Technology Strategy Board started its own innovation vouchers in September 2012, as part of the government's strategy to generate growth through research and innovation. Each year, it is offering a total of 400 vouchers worth £5,000, which it releases in rounds of a hundred each quarter.

Its initial focus was on projects in agri-food and the built environment. Energy, water and waste are next. Based on how the programme develops, other sectors will be included. A separate competition is already available for projects in space: 50 vouchers worth £8,000 are available each year through the International Space Innovation Centre.

Applications are designed to be as easy as possible. As long as you are clear on your aims, the online form is expected to take 30 minutes to complete. Once it is clear that you are an SME tackling a challenge that requires you to bring in specialist help for the first time, your application will enter a random draw, thereby giving everyone a fair chance. If your name is selected, you then carry out the project with your knowledge partner. If you are happy with their work, you then forward the invoice to the TSB for settlement.

For further details see: http://vouchers.innovateuk.org

Appendix 2

Knowledge Transfer Networks

Ever wished you could improve the chances of bumping into the right expert at the right time? Or know when competitions or tenders relevant to you are due to open? Even influence the direction of policy towards your area of technology?

Then it could be worth taking a look at Knowledge Transfer Networks (KTNs). They are designed to drive the flow of knowledge round 15 major disciplines within innovation. Members are drawn from a broad cross-section of business, research and government, including many experts within universities.

Each KTN carries information, contacts and insights within its area of specialisation. They are run by the Technology Strategy Board (TSB) and the assumption is that everything is available on the basis of shared knowledge and open innovation.

As well as pointing you towards the right expert and bringing you up to speed on the next round of funding opportunities, the KTNs act as a sounding board for where support for technology might best be directed next.

The networks cover the following disciplines:

- aerospace, aviation and defence
- biosciences
- chemistry innovation
- creative industries
- electronics, sensors, photonics
- energy generation and supply
- environmental sustainability
- financial services
- health tech and medicines
- information and communications technology
- industrial mathematics
- materials

- modern built environment
- nanotechnology
- transport.

All told, these 15 KTNs have 30,000 members, who, taken as a whole, are well placed to have a crack at solving most technical challenges that a business might encounter. They also represent a potentially powerful force in working across disciplines, which is often where the most innovative ideas are found.

To facilitate a speedy crossover of ideas, the KTNs all operate on a single interlinked platform (_connect) under the auspices of the TSB. As a business user, the intention is to let you discuss challenges, find partners and build collaborations. You can join _connect for free at ktn.innovateuk.org.

Further details about KTNs can be found at: www.innovateuk.org/connect

Appendix 3

Knowledge Transfer Partnerships

Knowledge Transfer Partnerships (KTPs) are a mechanism for applying a university's expertise to the challenges that a business is facing in developing an innovative solution. A new product, a new service or a new process might be the result.

The idea is that knowledge transfer is about more than signing an agreement. It generally works best when you can bring in someone to make it happen. It takes time to turn theoretical expertise into commercial applications.

Such interactions between those in research and those in business can act as a powerful stimulant. One maker of caravans in East Yorkshire took its sales up from £6m to £20m by bringing in engineers from the University of Hull to improve its design when it decided to move into the market for holiday lodges.

Typically, such assignments last for one to three years. A graduate is recruited and employed by the university, but will then work full time in your business under the supervision of a senior academic.

As an enterprise, you meet a third of the costs. The rest is covered by a fund organised centrally through the Technology Strategy Board (TSB).

For SMEs, there is an option to run shorter programmes of 10 to 40 weeks, although you can review your involvement after three months on longer programmes. After a recent confirmation that the KTPs will continue as an integral part of the government's commitment to accelerating innovation, you can also qualify to pay 25% instead of 33% of the cost.

The scheme has been running for over 30 years and typically funds well over a thousand projects a year. All forms of commercial activity are included. As well as product development, examples include software development, brand strategy, process improvement and data analysis.

Any size of business can take part, although those who employ between 10 and 50 people are the most active participants, accounting for 37% of the total. For SMEs, the calculation is often made that the cost of a KTP is significantly lower than recruiting a new member of staff directly. As well as bringing a researcher into the business to work on a problem for you, you gain access to the university's knowledge of your field as a whole.

Overall, the TSB calculates that every pound it spends on KTPs results in a £3.08 rise in the pre-tax profits forecast by participating companies. Or put it another way. On average, the thousand companies in the KTP portfolio improve their profits by between £240,000 and £290,000.

The performance of any individual project depends on finding an enthusiastic academic who is working in a field of knowledge closely allied to your own. In combination, you then have to find the right researcher, who will typically be a postgraduate, to spearhead the project. For them it is a chance to apply their knowledge on a live project and to advance their career. Once the project is finished, 75% are subsequently offered a permanent post by their host company.

A positive outcome also depends on the university's active engagement and support. For it, KTPs are attractive because they speed up the transfer of knowledge, create a new line of income, open up new lines of inquiry for future research, give more opportunities to graduate students, establish a powerful bond with a commercial partner and strengthen the practical dimension in what it is teaching. As one academic commented, "it shows our students that we are operating in the real world".

Further details: www.ktponline.org.uk

Appendix 4
CASE awards

Originally known as Collaborative Awards in Science and Engineering, the CASE scheme is now more widely pursued through all the research councils. The awards are designed to encourage and support postgraduates to pursue research projects for their doctorates which are jointly devised and supervised by a university and by a partner in business.

For a smaller company, it can be an attractive way of gaining access to high-level knowledge and skills at a heavily discounted, or even fully subsidised, cost.

For students, it opens up the chance of working on a question of immediate relevance and improving their commercial experience. As part of their studies over three years, they are expected to spend at least three months in the workplace. Some spend much more time on site.

Typically, as a business, your commitment will be to make some input to the research, then contribute at least £1,400 a year towards your academic partners and £2,500 towards the student's income.

However, if you qualify as an SME under the EU's definition (your headcount is fewer than 250 and your turnover is less than €50m), then the research council will generally pick up all these costs.

Further details from Research Councils UK: www.rcuk.ac.uk/connect

Appendix 5

Model agreements for university–business research collaboration

Templates and models for intellectual property

The Intellectual Property Office offers several templates and model agreements to assist industry–university collaboration.

The Lambert Toolkit, built on the collective experience of the UK's technology transfer community, offers a set of model agreements. Each provides a different approach in key areas of who owns, and has the right to exploit, the intellectual property in the results of the collaborative project. There are five Model Research Collaboration Agreements (One to One) and a Decision Guide to help choose the right agreement. Most commonly used is Lambert Agreement 1 (university owns the IP and gives industry a non-exclusive licence to use it). Lambert Agreement 4 represents the opposite relationship and is usually used where the industry party provides the major funding resource to the project. Lambert Agreement 5 covers contract research where industry owns the IP and the university retains no rights to publish research without the sponsor's permission. In Lambert Agreements 2 and 3 the university owns the IP for which industry can negotiate an exclusive licence or an assignment to exploit.

None of the five Research Collaboration Agreements deals with joint ownership of IP because this occurs more rarely than people think and is more difficult for both industry and the university to manage. However, of the four Lambert Model Consortium Agreements (Multi-Party), Consortium Agreement A contains an example of a joint ownership provision. It is important that the Agreement sets out what rights each joint owner has to exploit the IP. The four Lambert Model Consortium Agreements reflect the same structure as the five Research Agreements, but contain additional provisions to cover some of the complications that arise as a result of having more than two parties.

The IPO also offers template examples of other agreements such as:

- a Patent Assignment (for example, where industry and the university reach agreement under Lambert Agreement 3 that the university will assign IP in certain results of research collaboration to industry)

- a Consultancy Agreement (for example, when an individual researcher undertakes to provide consultancy services to a commercial sponsor).

The five Lambert Model Agreements (LMA) for research collaboration

LMA	Terms	IP owner
1	Business has non-exclusive rights to use in specified field of technology and/or geographical territory; no sub-licences	University
2	Business may negotiate further licence to some or all university IP	University
3	Business may negotiate for an assignment of some university IP	University
4	University has right to use for non-commercial purposes	Business
5	Contract research: no publication by university without business's permission	Business

The Lambert Model Consortium Agreements (LMCA)

Lambert Model Consortium Agreement	Terms
Agreement A	Each member of the Consortium owns the IP in the Results that it creates and grants each of the other parties a non-exclusive licence to use those Results for the purposes of the Project and for any other purpose.
Agreement B	The other parties assign their IP in the Results to the lead Exploitation Party who undertakes to exploit the Results. (Alternatively the Lead Exploitation Party is granted an exclusive licence.)
Agreement C	Each party takes an assignment of IP in the Results that are germane to its core business and undertakes to exploit those Results.
Agreement D	Each member of the Consortium owns the IP in the Results that it creates and grants each of the other parties a non-exclusive licence to use those Results for the purposes of the Project only. If any member of the Consortium wishes to negotiate a licence to allow it to exploit the IP of another member or to take an assignment of that IP, the owner of that IP undertakes to negotiate a licence or assignment.

Other useful resources for business–university collaborations

	Resource	Example of when used
1	Sample Patent and Know-how Licence	Where the Sponsor and the University have reached agreement that the Sponsor should be granted an exclusive licence to use identified IP in the results of a research collaboration (see Lambert Model Agreement 2).
2	Sample Patent Assignment	Where the Sponsor and the University have reached agreement that the University will assign IP in certain Results of a research collaboration to the Sponsor (see Lambert Model Agreement 3). It is based on the assumption that the Assignee will pay a one-off sum for the assignment of the Patent, but the parties may agree revenue sharing or other payment terms.
3	Sample Materials Transfer Agreement	Where a Sponsor has agreed to allow the University to use certain materials in connection with a research project.
4	Sample Consultancy Agreement	Where there is an agreement between a commercial Sponsor and an individual academic researcher, under which the individual researcher undertakes to provide consultancy services to the Sponsor. It records a private arrangement between the researcher and the Sponsor. The researcher assigns the intellectual property rights in the work he does as a consultant to the Sponsor in return for payments made by the Sponsor. In order to be able to assign those rights, the researcher must own them. That normally means that they must not have been developed in the course of his or her employment by the university; if they have been developed in the course of his employment, those rights will usually belong to the university.
5	Sample Non-Disclosure Agreement	Where a Business and a University wish to exchange confidential information as part of their discussions about a potential research project before they have entered into a Collaboration Agreement.
6	Sample Equipment Loan Agreement	Where the Business Sponsor has agreed to allow the University to use equipment in connection with a research project.
7	Sample Confidentiality Notice	A simple example of the kind of notification a user would include on the front page of a document to indicate that it and the information provided are confidential.

Further details: www.ipo.gov.uk/lambert

Appendix 6
The support network

The **Technology Strategy Board** (TSB) is the UK's national innovation agency. Its goal is to accelerate economic growth by stimulating and supporting business-led innovation. It works right across government, business and the research community – removing barriers to innovation, bringing organisations together to focus on opportunities, running competitions for research, and investing in the development of new technology-based products and services for future markets. Further details: www.innovateuk.org.

The **Intellectual Property Office (IPO)** is the official government body responsible for Intellectual Property (IP) rights in the United Kingdom. These rights include trade marks, patents, designs and copyright. The IPO offers a range of products and services to support businesses; these include an IP Healthcheck diagnostic tool, a range of free booklets, newsletters, workshops and seminars. Further details: www. ipo.gov.uk or 0300 300 2000.

Research Councils UK (RCUK) is the strategic partnership of the UK's seven research councils. They invest annually around £3bn in research. Their focus is on excellence with impact. They nurture the highest quality research, as judged by international peer review, providing the UK with a competitive advantage. Global research requires we sustain a diversity of funding approaches, fostering international collaborations, and providing access to the best facilities and infrastructure, and locating skilled researchers in stimulating environments. Their research achieves impact – the demonstrable contribution to society and the economy made by knowledge and skilled people. To deliver impact, researchers and businesses need to engage and collaborate with the public, business, government and charitable organisations. Further details: www.rcuk.ac.uk.

Universities UK (UUK) is the representative body for the executive heads of UK universities and is recognised as the umbrella group for the university sector. It works to advance the interests of universities and to spread good practice throughout the higher education sector. Universities UK is a company limited by guarantee with charitable status. UUK members are the executive heads (Vice-Chancellors or Principals) of UK universities and colleges of higher education. UUK currently has 133 members. Further details: www.universitiesuk.ac.uk.

PraxisUnico is the UK's leading association for research commercialisation professionals, working as an educational not-for-profit organisation set up to support innovation and commercialisation of public sector and charity research for social and economic impact. PraxisUnico encourages innovation and acts as a voice for the research commercialisation profession, facilitating the interaction between the public sector research base, business and government. PraxisUnico provides a forum for best practice exchange, underpinned by first-class training and development programmes. Further details: www.praxisunico.org.uk.

Interface – the knowledge connection for business – is a matchmaking service connecting businesses quickly and easily to world-class expertise, knowledge and research facilities available in Scotland's universities and research institutes. Interface's free and impartial service stimulates innovation and encourages companies to consider academic support to help solve their business challenges. Open to all, regardless of sector or geographical location, Interface proves that collaborating with academic partners brings significant business benefits including increased competitiveness, the introduction of a new product or service and company expansion. If you have a specific business challenge – technical, process or strategic, Interface will help you access the knowledge and facilities available from Scotland's universities and research institutes. To find out more and view client case studies, visit www.interface-online.org.uk or email info@interface-online.org.uk.

AURIL (Association for University Research and Industry Links) is the professional association representing all practitioners involved in knowledge creation, development and exchange in the UK and Ireland who work to ensure that new ideas, technologies and innovations flow from their institution into the marketplace. It is the largest knowledge transfer association in Europe, with more than 1,600 members from universities, NHS Trusts and public sector research establishments. The Association enjoys widespread international recognition through its success in influencing UK government policy. It has strong working relations with the Confederation of British Industry, Universities UK, the UKIPO, the Department for Business, Innovation & Skills (BIS), HM Treasury and Higher Education Funding Councils, in partnership with which it has produced many publications. Further details: www.auril.org.uk.

The **Institute of Knowledge Transfer (IKT)** is the sector's body devoted to supporting and promoting the profession of knowledge transfer, fostering greater understanding of knowledge transfer and enhancing the status of those involved in the profession. It is dedicated solely to meeting the needs of the individuals involved in knowledge transfer; the professionals which make this dynamic new industry. The IKT will set standards for development of the profession and address issues surrounding accreditation, certification and training. Further details: www.ikt.org.uk.

The **Department for Business, Innovation & Skills (BIS)** brings all of the levers of the economy together in one place and its policy areas can all help to drive growth. Among its aims:

- it is committed to fostering world-class higher education to provide the nation with the high level skills needed for economic success, while ensuring excellence in teaching and research

- it intends to create a high quality and responsive further education sector that equips workers with the skills demanded in a modern globalised economy

- it pursues global excellence in science and research to help maintain economic prosperity and address key global and domestic challenges, such as climate change and security

- it leads on the innovation agenda and is taking action to boost innovation in the economy and across the public sector, because it helps deal with complex challenges and drive growth by improving productivity and R&D.

Further details: www.bis.gov.uk.

The **Higher Education Funding Council for England (HEFCE)** distributes public money for research and teaching to universities and colleges in England that provide higher education. In doing so, it aims to promote high quality education and research, within a financially healthy sector. The Council also plays a key role in ensuring accountability and promoting good practice. HEFCE was set up by the government in 1992 as a "non-departmental public body". HEFCE's funds support four main areas of activity by universities and colleges as set out in the Council's strategic aims, one of which is the contribution of HE to the economy and society. Under this head, HEFCE, jointly with the Office of Science and Innovation, allocates the Higher Education Innovation Fund (HEIF) which supports business and community engagement and knowledge exchange. Further details: www.hefce.ac.uk.

The **Scottish Funding Council (SFC)** is the national, strategic body that is responsible for funding teaching and learning provision, research and other activities in Scotland's 41 colleges and 19 universities and higher education institutions. Its mission is to invest in the development of a coherent college and university system which, through enhanced learning, research and knowledge exchange, leads to improved economic, educational, social, civic and cultural outcomes for the people of Scotland. Further details: www.sfc.ac.uk.

The **Higher Education Funding Council for Wales (HEFCW)** is the Welsh Government's agency for distributing funding for higher education in Wales. Its objectives are to develop and sustain internationally excellent higher education in Wales, for the benefit of individuals, society and the economy, in Wales and more widely. Resources are deployed to secure HE learning and research of the highest quality, make the most of the contribution of HE to Wales's culture, society and economy and ensure high quality, accredited teacher training. Further details: www.hefcw.ac.uk.

Northern Ireland's **Department for Employment and Learning** promotes economic, social and personal development through high quality learning, research and skills training. Its four priorities are as follows.

- Enhancing the provision of learning and skills, including entrepreneurship, enterprise, management and leadership.

- Increasing the level of research and development, creativity and innovation in the Northern Ireland economy.

- Helping individuals to acquire jobs, including self-employment, and improving the linkages between employment programmes and skills development.

- The development and maintenance of the framework of employment rights and responsibilities.

Further details: www.delni.gov.uk.

NESTA is the National Endowment for Science, Technology and the Arts, an independent body with a mission to make the UK more innovative. It invests in early-stage companies, informs policy, and delivers practical programmes that inspire others to solve the big challenges of the future. Further details: www.nesta.org.uk.

National Centre for Entrepreneurship in Education (NCEE) is focused on graduates starting businesses, and on understanding, developing and promoting a culture of entrepreneurship within Higher Education through research, education and facilitation. Further details: www.ncee.org.uk.

The **National Association of College & University Entrepreneurs (NACUE)** is a national organisation that supports and represents university enterprise societies and student entrepreneurs to drive the growth of entrepreneurship across the UK. Further details: www.nacue.com.

Appendix 7
Further reading

Encouraging a British Innovation Revolution: Sir Andrew Witty's Review of Universities and Growth, Department for Business, Innovation & Skills, October 2013 (www.gov.uk/bis)

Commercialising Public Research: New Trends and Strategies, OECD, 2013

Creating Markets from Research Results, EPO, 2013 (www.epo.org)

IP Insight, an e-newsletter from the Intellectual Property Office on developments in IP (www.ipo.gov.uk/newsletters)

A Review of Business-University Collaboration, Professor Sir Tim Wilson DL, Department for Business, Innovation & Skills, February 2012 (www.gov.uk/bis)

Innovation Report, 2010, Department for Business, Innovation & Skills/NESTA (www.gov.uk/bis)

The Wider Conditions for Innovation in the UK: how the UK compares to leading innovation nations, NESTA, 2009 (www.nesta.org.uk)

Higher Ambition: future of universities in the knowledge economy, Department for Business, Innovation & Skills, 2009. Executive summary at: www.bis.gov.uk/assets/biscore/corporate/docs/h/09-1452-higher-ambitions-summary.pdf

The Future of Research, Universities UK, 2010

The Edgeless University: why higher education must embrace technology, P. Bradwell, Demos, 2009, www.demos.co.uk/publications/the-edgeless-university

Knowledge Exchange: insider special report in association with Interface, 2010, www.interface-online.org.uk/3930

(Un)common Ground: creative encounters across sectors and disciplines, Virtueel Platform, 2007, wwww.virtueelplatform.nl

Understanding Work-Based Learning, edited by Simon Roodhouse and John Mumford, Gower, 2010

Reports on Intellectual Property and Research Benefits for the Secretary of State for Innovation, Universities and Skills, Professor Paul Wellings, Lancaster University, September 2008

New Light on Innovation, Engineering Employers Federation, 2006, www.eef.org.uk

High Growth Firms in Scotland, C. Mason and R. Brown, Hunter Centre for Entrepreneurship, University of Strathclyde and Scottish Enterprise, June 2010

PART 7

University Profiles

CHECK IN, START UP AND SPIN OUT
AT ANGLIA RUSKIN

Modern universities no longer solely focus on research and educating and developing the individual; they now have a vital role in developing local businesses and driving economic growth in their regions.

With campuses in three major cities – Cambridge, Chelmsford and Peterborough – Anglia Ruskin University is a catalyst for business growth. In the last 12 months, Anglia Ruskin has worked with more than 2,000 UK businesses and organisations, from giants such as Barclays, Specsavers and the British Army, through to entrepreneurs, early-stage start-ups and spin-outs. Many of these smaller businesses have never previously worked with a university.

Through established routes such as Knowledge Transfer Programmes, businesses can partner with our academics and researchers to improve processes or products or fast-track new innovations to market. We also help companies access and develop graduate talent through our recruitment and internship programme and have pioneered work-based degrees and innovative approaches to learning through professional courses.

Anglia Ruskin is particularly strong in the areas of Health and MedTech. The Postgraduate Medical Institute (PMI), for example, is a partnership of 22 key organisations including NHS Trusts, private healthcare providers, Essex County Council and the Royal Society of Public Health.

Through the PMI, Anglia Ruskin has been able to bring in inspirational leaders from the NHS, such as Professor Tony Young, who, as well as being a consultant surgeon, is a successful entrepreneur and champion for innovation.

We also work with private and public sector partners on the Anglia Ruskin MedTech Campus and The MedBIC, our new innovation centre for medical and advanced engineering in Chelmsford, Essex. Both projects are devoted to fostering growth and supporting new businesses in these sectors. Support can include access to funding opportunities, networking events, professional development, specialist equipment and facilities, our research centres and technical expertise.

To find out more about how Anglia Ruskin can support you to fast-track the development of your idea, innovation or business, get in touch:

Call: 0845 196 5878
Email: tom.bates@anglia.ac.uk
business.anglia.ac.uk

The MedBIC

Call: 0845 196 4207
Email: info@medbic.com
www.medbic.com

MedTech Campus

Call: 0845 196 3177
Email: info@medtechcampus.com
www.medtechcampus.com

Anglia Ruskin University

ONE PLACE
TO GROW YOUR BUSINESS

The MedBIC – Anglia Ruskin's Business Innovation Centre for Medical and Advanced Engineering – is made for start-ups and early-stage businesses in these sectors. It is purpose built to speed commercial ideas to market and nurture fledgling ventures by providing all the resources, expertise and support required in a single building. Centrally located in Chelmsford, Essex, The MedBIC is run by Anglia Ruskin University and supported by industry and local government.

The co-operative workspaces and start-up focused programmes at The MedBIC can make entrepreneurial visions a reality. This is alongside supportive academics, researchers, consultants and clinicians who can assist with prototyping, clinical trials and testing – all aimed at speeding up routes to market.

Working with occupant companies and a wide range of sector-focused industry partners and experts, The MedBIC offers access to funding, markets and technology through a range of commercial, technical and business support services. Occupants can also access Anglia Ruskin's wider research and innovation support.

If you're considering setting up a business, The MedBIC is a professional and comfortable setting for businesses to be developed, with the support of like-minded individuals. This industry-driven space encourages open innovation and knowledge transfer, offering new businesses the space to grow and expand, with all the support needed to ensure success.

There are a range of membership packages available to suit all business needs. Whether it's dedicated desks or office space, the occasional use of a desk away from home, or a prestigious business address, we can help you grow your idea or business.

"As a newly-established business, being able to work in partnership with Anglia Ruskin over the past few months has been a tremendous boost and we are really looking forward to working out of The MedBIC. Having access to the facilities and expertise will help us provide a much better service for our clients and will be vital to growing our business. We're delighted to be on-board."

Mike Jefferson, Director of The Specialist Health Centre, has seen his seven-strong team become The MedBIC's first tenants, while also working with Anglia Ruskin's Postgraduate Medical Institute (PMI) to access its Clinical Trials Unit.

The MedBIC | **Anglia Ruskin University**

Business Innovation Centre, Medical and Advanced Engineering

Get in touch:
Call: 0845 196 4207
Email: info@medbic.com
www.medbic.com

Sharing expertise to build success

BIRMINGHAM CITY
University

Birmingham City University is committed to helping businesses develop and grow – from the smallest SMEs to leading brands such as Rolls-Royce, Cisco, Microsoft and Codemasters. From the engineering and automotive sectors to the creative industries, we make a significant contribution to business by sharing and embedding our own academic expertise and graduate talent.

Innovation is at the centre of our work with business, industry and other outside organisations. This is typified through our involvement in the Knowledge Exchange and Enterprise Network (KEEN), a business improvement programme, part-funded by ERDF, and designed specifically to help West Midlands based SME's increase their profitability and achieve growth through working with a regional university.

By sharing our ideas and expertise, and allowing best practice to be shared across the West Midlands region and further afield, we help our partners to achieve success. In turn, our students benefit from the chance to work at close quarter with these partners and by studying on courses which have been designed with employers' needs in mind.

Our promotion of innovation can take many forms, from providing original solutions to real-life problems, to designing bespoke courses that meet the needs of business.

For example, leading outdoor furniture manufacturer Hartman UK collaborated with us to find the next generation of designers who could give a new twist to outdoor living. Working with the academic teams of our Product/Interior Design and Textile Design courses, Hartman launched their 2012/13 competition for 24 BA (Hons) Product/Interior Design students and 79 BA (Hons) Textile Design students to create new product and fabric concepts for outdoor furniture.

Birmingham City University is also one of two providers for the BBC's new technology and engineering apprentice scheme, the BBC Technology Apprenticeship. Students on the scheme will qualify as a Bachelors of Engineer (BEng) in Broadcast Engineering at the end of t programme, setting them up to compete for job at the BBC or across the industry.

A new specialist postgraduate management development programme, Leaders in Leisure, was developed in conjunction with Birmingham City Business School (BCBS), part of the University, and launched by leading leisure business The Rank Group plc. The qualification delivered primarily by the experienced BCBS team, with specialist input from Rank Group experts.

Our Research, Innovation and Enterprise department (RIE) established a strategic partnership with the new Library of Birmingha in preparation for the opening of Europe's large and most ambitious public library project in 20 The partnership has yielded a number of relationships for the University, including work experience for 12 volunteers and a performanc by musicians from Birmingham Conservatoire the opening event.

We produce skilled and employable students a graduates, offering industry-inspired recruitm and selection services to ensure businesses ge the right candidate. This has resulted in 90 per cent of graduates entering employment or furth study within six months of graduation (Destinations survey 2011/12). Over the past 10 years, we have worked with over 5,000 SMEs a our continued success is testimony to our supp of, and commitment to, smaller businesses.

For more information, contact:
Research, Innovation and Enterprise Services
Tel: 0121 331 5252
Email: business.services@bcu.ac.uk
Web: www.bcu.ac.uk/business

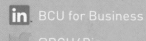

in. BCU for Business

@BCU4Biz

Case study

orking in partnership to design new concept vehicle

-gan Motor Company Ltd, the renowned manufacturer of hand-built sports cars, operates on a
bal scale, and after 100 years of continuous operation is still owned by the same family. The
npany specialises in the design, manufacture and distribution of exclusive sports cars into the
n-value performance market sectors.

:ompete in today's challenging economic climate, it is vital that Morgan continuously improves and
ovates in its operations. Building on the success of previous collaborations with Birmingham City
versity, the firm initiated a Knowledge Transfer Partnership (KTP) to develop a new concept
icle.

:thew Humphries, already working in the business on a student placement, was recruited as an
.ociate for a Knowledge Transfer Partnership between Morgan, Birmingham City University and
er universities. He worked with the Morgan team to develop the AeroMax concept, intended to
nulate the market and attract new customers to the brand.

: new design process has helped to ensure that design details are cost-effective and fully
ropriate for the Morgan production processes. Its efficacy was proven in taking the AeroMax from
cept prototype to low volume production, delivering a vehicle that offers a major leap forward for
company in terms of quality and design detail. All 100 of the cars were pre-sold, which generated
million in revenues and £2 million profits, representing a 24 per cent return on investment.

ing 2010, the value of a decade of knowledge transfer programmes between Morgan and
mingham City University was recognised as regional winner for 'Best Partnership – North West',
he KTP Awards. Prior to this, the partnership saw Morgan gain a Lord Stafford Award for
ievement in Innovation in 2007.

llaborations between universities and
inesses are essential – what better way than
ough Knowledge Transfer Partnerships
ere businesses gain a graduate committed to
eloping a key project in your company and
nging with them the knowledge within their
versities to drive growth and success more
ckly," said Natalie Lewis, Birmingham City
versity's Knowledge Transfer Manager.

ase contact Natalie Lewis on
1 331 5677 or send an email to
alie.lewis@bcu.ac.uk to discuss how
owledge Transfer Partnerships or our
olvement in the regional Knowledge
hange and Enterprise Network (KEEN)
gramme could benefit your business.

BCU for Business

@BCU4Biz

UNIVERSITY of
BRADFORD

Gain access to leading-edge facilities and academic experts through our Schools and Centres who can help you design and redesign your product rang services and infrastructure to give you competitive edge.

Our Business Partnerships Team work to help you pinpoint an expert or area within the University and advise on what intervention would fit best with the work you need doing wheth that's networking, consultancy, a student placement, a research project, or bespoke training and development or qualification packages for your staff.

We can access Technology Strategy Board (TSB) funding for yo including research and development grants, innovation vouche and Knowledge Transfer Partnerships.

We work with all types of organisation, small to large across the globe. We work regularly with startups, micro businesses and SMEs and have also worked with some of the world's biggest brands such as Dyson, Boots, Bupa and Ford. Hundreds of SME are accessing our services at any one time.

Our academic expertise is focussed around 3 themes: Healthca Science; Innovative Engineering; and People and Society. Withi these themes we have many specialist individuals, research groups and interdisciplinary Research and Knowledge Transfer Centres offering business services.

We are a research active institution with almost

50 years

of experience.

80%

of our research was rated either 'international' or 'world-leading'* *(RAE)*

* Research Assessment Excercise.

ır main campus is nestled in the heart of the City making it easy
do business with us. Our campus facilities complement our
ıople expertise with world-class teaching and research spaces.

ıe Business Partnerships Team are based in the new £6m
ıtstanding BREEAM rated Bright Building, the University's new
ınt door for business with meeting and seminar space and
xible and collaborative office space for SMEs. The building is
o home to the University's Re:centre. In a beautiful setting
ıtside the City, we also have Heaton Mount – a bookable
ırpose-built conference facility.

:centre is part financed by the European Union. The project has
ıracted £2.7 million from the European Regional Development
ıd the Yorkshire and Humber ERDF Programme 2007-13. The
ıntre has also attracted funding from the Higher Education
ıding Council for England.

NORGREN

ırgren is a global engineering company offering engineering
sign solutions. The School of Engineering and Informatics
ırked with them to provide an understanding of the detailed
chanical, fluid and material principles of Norgren's existing
rrent to Pressure (I/P) converter leading to the design of a
w generation of products.

Sovereign
Health Care Charitable Trust

ıvereign Health Care are an independent, not-for-dividend
ınpany who provide health cash plans to individuals and
ınpanies. They worked with the University of Bradford's School
ınformatics on a Knowledge Transfer Partnership (KTP) to
ıbed an organisation wide e-strategy to process healthcare
ıims, manage healthcare policies and communicate with
ıtomers and employees electronically.

siness Partnerships Team
01274 236000
rkts@bradford.ac.uk
@bradfordimpact
www.bradford.ac.uk/business

EUROPEAN UNION
Investing in Your Future
European Regional
Development Fund 2007-13

A technology
University offering
business solutions
supported by
world-leading facilities
and expertise in the
Centre of Bradford.

The Bradford
Distance-Learning
MBA is ranked

11th

in the World*

* Online MBA rankings,
Financial Times, 10 March 2014

We work with over

500

businesses per year

The University of Cambridge
Cambridge Enterprise

University of Cambridge people and ideas are at the heart of the Cambridge Phenomenon, one of the world's most productive technology clusters. The economic, social and environmental impact of these companies and the people they attract are evident everywhere.

Cambridge Enterprise, a wholly owned subsidiary of the University, is responsible for commercialising Cambridge research. The company works in partnership with industry to ensure that Cambridge innovation has maximum societal and financial impact. We act as business agents for academics who wish to act as consultants, oversee the licensing of inventions and find vital funding opportunities for early-stage companies.

In the most recent national survey conducted in 2008, Cambridge Enterprise was ranked as the UK's top technology transfer office, and has been highly successful in bringing Cambridge research to the wider world, through consultancy, licensing and spin-out companies.

The sharing of University research leads to incredible advances in technology, bioscience and engineering, bringing huge benefits to society and making a direct impact on the economy by creating new jobs, attracting inward investment and generating sales.

Consultancy Services enables the University to share its knowledge with government, industry and the public sector, and make a direct impact on society. Our goal is to make the process of consultancy easier for academics and the organisations in need of their expertise. Our service covers the administrative issues associated with consultancy projects, including the negotiation of contract terms and conditions, arrangements for use of University facilities, invoicing, debt collection, and income distribution. Examples of the types of consultancy projects undertaken include: technical and creative solutions to specific business problems, provision of expert reports on technical, economic and commercial issues, expert witness advice and serving on scientific advisory boards.

Technology Transfer involves management and licensing of intellectual property, and provides access to proof of concept funding for the development of early stage inventions. Licensing Cambridge research to existing companies is the core of Cambridge Enterprise's business, and licensing has led to innumerable financial and societal benefits. Successes include the drug Alemtuzumab, which was marketed under the name Campath®, and is used as an effective treatment for chronic lymphocytic leukaemia. Alemtuzumab, also marketed as Lemtrada, was recently approved for use as a treatment for relapsing forms of multiple sclerosis; and CASTEP, a computer-based materials simulation toolkit which is used worldwide in a wide range of industries.

Cambridge Enterprise Seed Funds provides access to early stage capital through the three evergreen seed funds it manages on the University's behalf. This early stage capital and support is pivotal to success of new technology companies in what is often seen as a high-risk section of the investment spectrum. Since seed funding began in 1995, our portfolio companies have raised more than £1.25 billion in further investment and grant funding.

+44 (0)1223 760339
www.enterprise.cam.ac.uk

Using printed lasers to fight fraud

A new printing method that uses lasers to identify counterfeit goods has been developed by a University of Cambridge spin-out whose researchers say it could make products, from currency to pharmaceuticals, more resistant to fraud.

The technology, which uses innovative printed optical materials, was developed within the University's Electrical Engineering Division. The team, led by Dr Damian Gardiner, a physicist and engineer, have formed the company ilumink to commercialise the technology, which has gained the attention of industry worldwide.

The commercialisation effort received a boost thanks to the Royal Academy of Engineering Enterprise Fellowship Scheme award for Dr Gardiner, who is working closely with Cambridge Enterprise, the commercialisation arm of the University, to secure intellectual property and develop the seed investment case for the spin-out.

The new technology uses liquid crystal ink (made from molecules that form helical patterns) and can be inkjet printed onto nearly any surface. The printed images, which can be both complex and colourful, are then authenticated with a laser.

Inkjet printing provides a very precise level of control over the laser's pattern and colour combination. The technology allows different kinds of features to be created – ranging from simple hologram-like patterns designed for the general public to authenticate, through to those that are used for high-security and need expensive, specialised equipment.

Unlike traditional security holograms, which are fundamentally identical, the new printing method marries optical materials and inkjet printing in a way that creates unique images. Using a dedicated reader, the images emit pure laser light with a specific signature.

Because lasers can be printed onto all kinds of surfaces – plastic, paper, metal and glass, among them– the new technique could be used to authenticate a wide range of products. Fake pharmaceuticals are a particular concern globally.

"Every year, hundreds of thousands of people are sold fake pharmaceuticals under the mistaken belief that they will help them, while counterfeit products cost companies hundreds of billions of pounds," Gardiner said. "We think that our printed lasers could be used to protect both products and people."

The technology was made possible using basic grant funding from the Engineering and Physical Research Council (EPSRC) COSMOS projects, with subsequent funding for commercialisation from the Cambridge Innovation and Knowledge Centre (CIKC), the EPSRC Impact Acceleration Account, and funding from the Royal Academy of Engineering Enterprise Hub.

THE AME OF THE GAME

"The start of a new journey that is set to change the way we train our engineers of the future"

A £32m+ collaboration between Unipart Manufacturing and Coventry University looks set to change the way we train the engineers of the future. Working with Universities finds out more about the Institute for Advanced Manufacturing and Engineering (AME).

If you suggested ten years ago that UK manufacturing would be driving the economy out of recession, many economic experts would have questioned your sanity.

An industry depleted by high-profile closures and migration of work to low cost countries was in what appeared to be terminal decline and the focus for the country's growth was placed firmly in the hands of the bankers and service sector.

We should have had more faith. Faced with adversity our firms have bounced back, focusing on what we do best... design, innovation and engineering solutions. This, along with a genuine shift to reshoring, has seen UK manufacturing become the new flavour of the month, with growth on the horizon and record levels of investment and job creation predicted.

The latter was brought sharply into focus by the Manufacturing Advisory Service's Barometer earlier this year, which revealed that more than 54% of manufacturing SMEs questioned were looking to recruit in the next twelve months. With popularity comes challenges and the well publicised 'skills shortage' is at the top of the agenda.

It is estimated that 82,000 engineers, scientists and technologists will need to be recruited and trained in the UK by 2017, with 363,000 of the current technical workforce qualified below world-class standards.**

These are figures Dr Carl Perrin knows only too well. In his role as Director of the Institute for Advanced Manufacturing and Engineering (AME), he has a rare opportunity to address some of these issues head on. The chartered engineer will be responsible for driving the launch of the UK's first 'Faculty on the Factory Floor', a £32m+ collaboration between Unipart Manufacturing and Coventry University that is part funded by the Higher Education Funding Council for England's Catalyst Fund.

The vision is to pioneer a higher education and research model for delivering manufacturing engineering degrees and new technologies, offering innovative learning by industry rofessionals, lecturers and professors... all delivered on live Unipart Manufacturing projects.

"We are at the start of a new journey, an exciting journey that could change the way we train our engineers of the future," explained Carl, who was previously Head of Technology in a joint venture at Rolls Royce and R&D Director at Dana Glacier Vandervell.

"For too long we have been focused on meeting the academic requirements, which is all well and good as long as we also look at equipping students with actual hands-on shopfloor and research experience."

He continued: "We are continually hearing from manufacturers that when they take on graduates they are not industry ready and it takes years for them to get up to speed so they can positively contribute to the bottom line.

"At AME we intend to put this right by giving our students access to Unipart Manufacturing experts, the best academic minds, researchers and state-of-the-art technology.

"What they learn will be applied immediately on the shopfloor to existing and future products that will be leaving the factory for customers all over the world."

It's an ambitious vision and one Carl doesn't take lightly. Pragmatism is one of his attributes. He points to the experience and strength of the two organisations – Unipart Manufacturing and Coventry University – as reason for believing this unique collaboration could be the sign of things to come.

"Doing something different always carries a certain element of risk, but I'm confident that the people driving it have the necessary knowledge and expertise to make it happen."

Carl is quick to point out that AME has also developed a 1700 sq metre dedicated hub for teaching and research housed on Unipart Eberspächer's site in Coventry.

"This will form the focal point of activity and will house state-of-the-art robotic automation, forming, joining, analysis and simulation, metrology and product verification technology. We're spending in excess of £2m on equipment and this is just the start."

AME has already welcomed its first cohort of undergraduates and postgraduates.

They are studying towards BEng, MEng (Hons) or MSc qualifications, with the opportunity to apply for industry internships, company placements and possible employment at Unipart globally or across its supply chain.

Students will have the opportunity to learn essential science and technology needed for today's professional engineer, how to solve design and manufacturing issues and use cutting-edge software to model, analyse and validate processes and systems.

The aim is to future proof engineers so they not only have the skills to make a difference now, but also in years to come.

Creating a pipeline of skilled engineering graduates is just one part of the AME offer," continued James Simester, who moved from Jaguar Land Rover to take up the position of Technology Director at AME.

We are also looking to attract and deliver cutting edge research projects that will drive forward the UK's global competitive advantage in fuel systems and powertrain for automotive, aerospace, power generation, rail and oil & gas.

Our purpose built facility will be the hub of the research activity and will provide an environment that will allow respected professors, researchers and industry professionals to work together on metrology, manufacturing systems, mechanical systems and design.

"All of the processes and solutions we develop will be disseminated for the benefit of the Unipart Manufacturing supply chain and wider UK industry as a whole."

He went on to add: "The plan is to attract funding by targeting support from strategic partners like the EU Commission, the Engineering and Physical Sciences Research Council (EPSRC) and the Technology Strategy Board (TSB)."

It's an approach that is already working. The first two major research projects are focusing on the development of new fuel rails and a virtual exhaust prototyping system.

The latter – called 'Towards Zero Prototyping' – involves developing a new modeling solution that will reduce the reliance on prototype components (e.g. exhausts), which can cost up to £100,000 per vehicle/powertrain variant.

The UK's first 'Faculty on the Factory Floor' has arrived. Industry will be watching to see if this 'game changing' approach to education and research has the desired impact on skills and the bottom line of domestic manufacturing.

For more information, visit **www.ame.co.uk**
Follow AME on twitter **@ame_uk**

** Source: SEMTA Facts and Figures

Profile

Durham University

Durham University has a proven track record of engaging with large and small business, public sector organisations, social enterprises and charities to nurture innovation and growth and ensure successful commercialisation of its own world class research.
It is a compact, research-intensive Russell Group university ranked 6th in the UK (The Times 2014) and is a world "Top-100" university.

Durham Business and Innovation Services (DBIS), the university's experienced frontline team, facilitates and manages engagement with local, national and international organisations. It comprises two groups working to deliver maximum benefits to business, non-commercial partners and academics.

The **Business Engagement Team** focuses on developing new, mutually-beneficial, long-term partnerships with a wide range of organisations, including SME's and social enterprises.

The **Research Commercialisation Team** focuses on the commercialisation of research outputs, handling patents, licensing and the formation of spin-out companies.

A prime example of Durham University's successful collaboration with business is its partnership with fast moving consumer goods giant Procter and Gamble (P&G).
This partnership has already secured more than £5.7 in Regional Growth Funding which has established a Surface Science Collaboration Centre, delivering multiple research projects of direct commercial relevance. Other activities include projects with Durham's Biophysical Sciences Institute, multi-partner research collaborations, tailored undergraduate courses, student enterprise and science outreach.
The success of this partnership was recognised formally when the university won the Global Business Development University Partner of the Year from P&G in 2011 and then won a P&G Strategic Partnership Award in November 2013.
Durham University, working with its partners, ensures high-tech innovative businesses in the North East are supported from conception through to realisation, incubation and rapid growth.

Tim Hammond and David Hodgson received a P&G Strategic Partnership award on behalf of Durham University at a recent European Innovation meeting in Brussels. The photograph shows (from left to right) Euan Magennis, Elena Lurieluke, Tim Hammond, David Hodgson, Michael Duncan and David Jakubovic.

Case Study

Durham University

IBEX Innovations

IBEX Innovations based in new facilities at Netpark, County Durham, employs a team of 8 highly experienced scientists, engineers and business professionals. It commercialises a patented X-ray imaging technology offering better contrast at far lower doses in a range of markets including Medical and Industrial Imaging. In 2012, IBEX Innovations received a METRC grant to collaborate with Professor David Wood, Chair of Engineering in the School of Engineering and Computing Sciences at Durham University.

In 2012, IBEX Innovations received a METRC grant to collaborate with Professor David Wood, Chair of Engineering in the School of Engineering and Computing Sciences at Durham University. IBEX Innovations had worked on new technology that would extract the spectral information in an X-ray beam when using indirect indicators. This would allow the identification of materials, allow exact thickness of the components in an image to be measured and increase early detection of cancers, amongst other things.

Professor Wood and his group worked on producing a structured plate to go in the x-ray beam. The collaboration also included Professor Andy Beeby's group which has expertise in luminescence spectroscopy. Professor Beeby helped in assessing the performance of different scintillators which could be chosen for devices.

IBEX Innovation's strong relationship with Durham University was further demonstrated with new research collaboration with Professor David Wooff's group in the Department of Mathematical Sciences. Dr Camila Caiado, Research Associate, used Bayesian analysis to optimise data analysis of the new X-ray detector.

In September 2013, the company announced that it has been successful in securing £250,000 from a Development of Prototype Smart grant awarded by the UK's innovation agency, the Technology Strategy Board.

The project is to develop X-ray detector prototypes for both Industrial Imaging and Medical Radiography applications. A major advantage of the technology is that it can be used to upgrade existing detectors and can be retro-fitted. It can be applied to a range of different industries such as Industrial NDT, Security and Medical Imaging.

In addition IBEX Innovation has also announced that it has signed a licencing agreement worth a minimum of £400,000 over 5 years. The first products incorporating IBEX's patented technology will be sold in 2014.

Following the award of the grant, both collaborations with Professor David Wood and Professor David Wooff will be extended in 2014 to contribute to the project. This will help significantly to develop a sustainable relationship between both organisations.

Dr.Gary Gibson, Chief Technology Officer commented:

"IBEX is working in some very advanced technology areas and our relationship with Durham University has been invaluable to us as we have developed our technology. The expertise and ingenuity of the academics at Durham has allowed us to make substantial leaps forward in our progress and helped to create some compelling advantages in our product offerings. I cannot stress strongly enough how useful the collaboration has proven to be to us."

The University of Hertfordshire is the UK's leading business-facing university and an exemplar in the sector. With a wealth of knowledge and expertise under one roof, the University can offer a wide range of tailored services to help you get measurable results for your business or organisation.

Knowledge Transfer

We have the technology and skills to enable businesses to embed new capabilities and improve business performance whilst encouraging innovation through skills diversification in the work place. Our Knowledge Transfer team have a distinguished track record in a range of partnerships with over 100 companies and have helped deliver projects in multiple areas including: low carbon automotive systems, operations management, health and wellbeing and sustainable/strategic marketing to name just a few.

Research and Development

Our research is innovative, relevant, highly applicable and easy to access for businesses. We offer tailored support to help accelerate opportunities in the following areas: contract research carried out on a subject defined by your business, grant-funded collaborative research into areas of joint interest and the chance to sponsor research students in an area of interest to your company.

Consultancy Services

Engage the expertise of the University of Hertfordshire to help develop your business solution. Get support and guidance by working closely with our academics on challenges which pose a problem within your organisation. Our consultants work extensively with clients in specialist areas including:

- business issues such as strategy
- marketing and statistics
- creative themes such as product design and media production
- environmental challenges such as: carbon reduction, water purity and resource efficiency
- engineering topics such as prototype production, materials testing and manufacturing and more.

Innovation Voucher Funding

The University of Hertfordshire can stimulate growth opportunities with funding support from our Innovation Voucher programme for SMEs and not for profit organisations which enables clients to double their project value to a maximum of £6000 whilst benefitting from an extensive range of expertise and facilities.

Market Research Service

Drawing upon expert knowledge of our respected academics and talented graduates, we deliver professional market and evaluation studies across diverse business sectors. We have delivered over 100 such projects to date, ranging from new product development to service evaluation for private, public and charitable organisations operating in local, national and international markets.

National Centre for Project Management

The National Centre for Project Management (NCPM) is an inter-disciplinary centre of excellence which operates in collaboration with industry, government, charities, NGOs and learned societies. The centre specialises in qualifications for working professionals in multiple sectors, advisory workshops on key management and leadership skills and competencies.

Contact us to find out more:
+ 44 (0) 1707 286406   be@herts.ac.uk   www.herts.ac.uk/businessservices

Fluorocarbon Limited KTP Case Study

Fluorocarbon Company are one of the UK's largest Fluoropolymer processors and global supplier of PTFE and polymer related components and semi-finished materials. Our customers are worldwide market leaders across many business/ industry areas. The Fluorocarbon Group business includes developing effective solutions with clients at the highest quality from material selection through to product design, manufacture and distribution.

Business Challenge

The company wanted to develop and embed lead manufacturing principles to enable process improvement, cost savings and efficiency gains. The 'business needs' driving the process improvements were to retain existing business and to attract new customers. The export market is a high level aspiration as part of the future expansion to provide high value specialist products with increased customer satisfaction. Development of staff skills was a necessary parallel action that was driven by the KTP Associate working with the workforce and developing supervisory skills.

How KTP helped

The KTP has, through various uses of business analysis tools, identified employees' skill gaps and education needs and provided and invested in the necessary requirements to bridge the gaps. It identified key priorities in each of our manufacturing areas, through the use of lean thinking and long term approach to competitiveness, providing individuals with basic problem solving tools. This enabled individuals to report based on management facts and provided knowledge sharing and vitality in a more collective environment. The KTP also assisted in the leadership of the company, through knowledge transfer, in the roll out and management of major cultural changes related to process improvements, improvements to the efficiency and effectiveness of the production process through implementing standard operation procedures and assisting the company with reducing costs. The reductions were achieved by providing the tools for identification, waste and non-value added activities in regards to materials, time, labour and quality. Management time has also been freed up from customer service and operation firefighting to allow full focus on business development and order generation by developing a trained workforce that are now capable of continually optimising the business process in a structured manner from the training provided.

Business Results

The KTP provided a platform for developing the profitable growth of the company by enabling us to utilise all the business processes and assisting the corporate objective of more than 18% return on capital employed. Along with this the KTP has developed the internal capabilities of the business creating value for Fluorocarbon's customers and within Fluorocarbon Group. This has been achieved by numerous factors set out in the overall objectives of the KTP that included identifying issues such as the establishment of process improvements in all areas of manufacturing and support, reducing overall cycle time. Value added activities were maximised with a reduced cycle time by removing buffering, rework, WIP and eliminating waste within the business processes. Business analysis tools, which now help in the supporting of business development decisions and communications for future prospects were also implemented and utilised in sections of the workforce. Development of our employees to create a can do-will do approach through identifying skills development in leaders, teams and individuals and providing support of education needs has also contributed to the Group strategy of embedding accountability, transparency and trust in key business areas.

University of
HUDDERSFIELD

University of Huddersfield

The University of Huddersfield works in partnership with businesses to provide access to our extensive knowledge, skills and resources

Creating Connections

We provide access to experienced researchers to help you resolve issues and develop business areas. We successfully match organisations with relevant multi-disciplinary expertise to create opportunities and help our partner organisations thrive.

Inspiring Innovation

We're experienced in creating diverse relationships with businesses, not-for-profit organisations and public sector bodies. We can work with you to form an innovative approach to accessing funding, addressing challenges and approaching research partnerships.

Developing People

When investing in staff development you want the best learning experience alongside value for money. We offer both off the shelf and bespoke Continuing Professional Development courses accredited by the University of Huddersfield.

Providing Facilities

The University invests in world-class facilities which can make a positive contribution to your success. We know how important it is to be at the cutting-edge of developments in research and teaching technologies, so the chances are we'll have the facilities to meet your needs.

We understand business needs and drivers and believe that effective collaboration requires familiarity, trust and confidence. We can work with you to define your interests and identify opportunities for collaboration, and in turn you can help inform our research.

Case Study – Paxman Coolers

Scalp cooling - a revolutionary treatment

One of the most obvious and distressing side-effects of chemotherapy is the hair loss suffered by most patients. Paxman Coolers Ltd manufactures scalp cooling equipment used worldwide to counter this effect but found that, despite significant empirical evidence of the efficacy of scalp cooling, uptake of the treatment was being hampered by a lack of clinical or biophysical studies that might explain the variable success rate.

Knowledge transfer partnership

The company joined in a Knowledge Transfer Partnership with the Schools of Applied Sciences and of Art, Design and Architecture to design an improved scalp cooling device and to establish a biologically-informed, evidence-based product development strategy.

Cutting-edge equipment

From the start, Paxman was clear about the targets it wanted to achieve and the University teams exceeded those expectations. Using anthropometric data, 3D scanning and laser sintering technology, the product design team's analysis and re-design of the existing cap produced several prototypes for testing.

Improving patient experiences

In addition to providing significant improvements in patient comfort and thermal conductivity, the team also developed a novel manufacturing system that promises to reduce costs and facilitate flexible production of the new design.

Improving products and processes

Paxman Coolers now has the capacity to accurately interpret clinical evidence in support of the efficacy of scalp cooling treatments and is developing a new cooling cap that is more comfortable for the patient, more effective in application and cheaper to mass produce.

"There was an absolutely productive relationship between all the partners. They are highly skilled academics but also completely understood the practical and business aspects of the project. In addition to providing the biological evidence to support scalp cooling treatments, the success of this project will enable us to develop better products and more accurate protocols for their application."

Patrick Burke, Technical Manager, Paxman Coolers

LIVERPOOL JOHN MOORES UNIVERSITY

Industry & Business Engagement at LJMU

Here at **Liverpool John Moores University** we are keen to make it simple for organisations to acces the knowledge base and expertise from any area of the University you want to work with.

Our core vision is 'To be recognised as a modern civic university delivering solution to the challenges of the 21st century'

Research & Innovation Services

LJMU's Research and Innovation Services Team is dedicated to provide a central point of contact to access the expertise and research capabilities across the university's range of disciplines. The Team's primary aim is to facilitate key collaborations to ensure we deliver the right solution to meet your needs.

The Team is experienced in the areas of Knowledge Exchange; Business Development, Accessing Grant Funding, Contract and Post Graduate Research and Commercialisation.

Some of the key routes for engagement:

- Contract/Collaborative Research
- Consultancy
- Knowledge Transfer Partnerships
- Bespoke training and development
- Facilitation services to support organisational change and strategic innovation

www.ljmu.ac.uk/business-engagement

t. 0500 876543
e. bdc@ljmu.ac.uk

Employer Engagement

The Employer Engagement team is designe to expand LJMU's connections with extern organisations by supporting employer relationship In liaison with the academic community the tear will actively seek out opportunities to develc mutually beneficial relationships between LJMU ar employers.

Some of the key services available for employers through this area are:

Advertising vacancies

Careers Fairs

Hosting Interviews

Presentations

Access to LJMU students

Support for work placement opportunities

For further Employer Engagement informatio please visit:

www.ljmu.ac.uk/worldofwork/Employers

We have top-rated, award-winning Knowledge Transfer Partnerships and unique collaborations that combine our academic skills with the real world know how of industry and business professionals

We offer a wide breadth of services to industry, business and external organisations and collaborate with of all sizes from start-ups to global blue chip organisations in both the public and private sectors.

ndustry Outreach projects

addition to Research & Innovation Services and e Employer Engagement team, LJMU currently erates three industry outreach projects dedicated foster activity within the local SME market.

hese sector hubs aim to stimulate and support ollaborations between businesses and LJMU d have specific focus covering the following eas:

reative & Digital Technologies - visit penLabs

ww.ljmu.ac.uk/aps/openlabs

ow Carbon - visit Low Carbon Innovation Hub

ww.ljmu.ac.uk/low-carbon

eneral Engineering - visit GERI

ww.ljmu.ac.uk/GERI

JMU's Industry Outreach projects are funded or art funded by the European Regional evelopment Fund.

Research Excellence

LJMU is one of the leading research-active contemporary institutions in the UK with 19 recognised Research Centres and Institutes

Our research has impact beyond academia, benefiting individuals, communities, industry & commerce and policy-makers throughout the UK and Worldwide.

Key discipline themes include:

- Astrophysics
- Health, Social Care, Informatics
- Criminalisation and Social Exclusion
- Computer Technology & Protection
- Engineering - General, Electrical, Mechanical & Materials
- Built Environment and Sustainable Technologies
- Logistics, offshore and Marine
- Physical Activity, Cardiovascular, Football and Sports Science
- Brain & Behaviour
- Cultural History, Urban Affairs & Environments
- Education

London South Bank University

Real Solutions for Real businesses

London South Bank University prides itself on being solution driven.

Drawing on world leading expertise and unique research capabilities the University is committed to delivering solutions that have a positive, concrete impact on individual organisations and society as a whole.

Over 150 major companies and SME's have formed research partnerships with us and we have completed over 160 Knowledge Transfer Partnerships with SME's in and around London, delivering a wide range of projects that have made a real difference.

These projects include:

Cooling the tube – working with Parsons Brinkerhoff to find innovative ways of using and improving technology to reduce temperatures on the tube. Key focuses of the project are the use of modelling/predictive software to mitigate excess heat and developing a better understanding of heat transfer in cooling pipes.

Reducing risk at Sellafield – improving the safety of nuclear decommissioning through better understanding of specific hydrogen issues.

Fitflop™ – LSBU's Sports and Exercise Science Research Centre assisted Fitflop™ with the development of the midsole technology which became the springboard for the now globally recognised brand Fitflop ™

Food for the future – as our population grows demands on our food resources will increase. Insects Au Gratin is a collaborative project that explores the nutritive and environmental aspects of the consumption of insects as food combined with 3D food printing technologies

Results-driven Relevant Training for your Employees

Around 30% of LSBU's students are employee sponsored - because we focus on developing relevant, vocational training for the modern market. We are helping over 1000 cross-sector industry partners to develop their workforce including GlaxoSmithKline, British Gas and Network Rail.

We design flexible, accredited courses that address your real world needs and skills gaps, drawing on genuine workplace situations and scenarios to ensure that sponsored students can benefit their organisations straight away.

Cutting Edge Facilities

We support our claim of being a highly applied University with exceptional and unique facilities designed to boost research and enterprise. We have invested over £60 million in our estate in the last 10 years alone. Facilities include:

The Pub Lab – LSBU's Psychology department's pub lab is used to understand addiction and why people drink in the way that they do.

The National Bakery School – a suite of rooms equipped to a professional standard for baking, confectionary making, chocolate making and fermenting.

The Clarence Centre for Enterprise and Innovation – a building dedicated to Enterprise where organisations, student businesses and University staff come together to foster success, create opportunity and innovate.

To explore the ways that LSBU can help your business email
b2b@lsbu.ac.uk **or telephone** 020 7815 6910.

London South Bank University

KNOWLEDGE TRANSFER PARTNERSHIPS

KTP Case Study –
Key20 Media

"Since we began our knowledge transfer partnership with LSBU we have made over 500 films and generated over £5 million in revenue. None of us expected this level of success."

Paul Richards, Managing Director, Key20 Media

LSBU helped media and communication experts Key20 Media to create an in-house production company helping the company to become a market leader in the digital space.

How the project started

Demand for web-hosted video has increased in the B2B sector, allowing organisations to convey complex business messages in a quick and accessible format. This presented an opportunity for Key20 Media but they needed a KTP with LSBU to make a good idea into a reality.

Before the KTP, Key20 outsourced video post-production, but this led to their having limited creative control and less flexibility. Engaging in a KTP with LSBU provided them the framework and expertise to build their own production studio, which reduced their reliance on external suppliers, and brought their creative control in-house.

Creating a New Capability

LSBU student and KTP Associate, Philip, set up a new production department 'Tracc Films' for Key20 that had the capabilities to shoot, edit, write and produce films. And Key20 didn't just have to rely on the talents of Philip as they discovered some hidden talents as their own staff bought into the project - an administrator doubling as a professional voiceover artist.

Tangible benefits quickly showed themselves as sales increased and Key20 were able to pitch for more complex projects. Philip set up an intern programme to meet this demand and added a valuable resource to the Key20 Media offer. They found that with the right training and engagement, graduates are spectacularly able, creative and productive. Now interns are regularly recruited.

A Platform for Growth

Initially the KTP led to £350,000 in savings for Key20 Media and expectations were that the new capability would result in £1,000,000+ impact on their bottom line over 2 years.

Tracc Films is currently making over 200 films a year resulting in £5 million+ in revenue since the project began.

Staff numbers in the production department have grown from 4 to 20 and Tracc films are focused on expanding their portfolio, strengthening existing relationships and seeking new clients.

To discuss a potential Knowledge Transfer Projects or to explore the other ways that LSBU can help your business email b2b@lsbu.ac.uk or telephone +44 (0)20 7815 6922

PROFILE

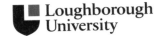
Loughborough University

Loughborough is one of the UK's top 20 universities – renowned for pioneering research that has an invaluable economic and social impact on the global, national and regional economy.

Our research expertise can enhance your organisation – making it leaner, greener and more profitable – helping to you solve your greatest challenges and stay ahead of the competition.

A range of global companies including adidas, BAE Systems, Caterpillar and Rolls-Royce as well as a host of SMEs already enjoy valuable partnerships with us. We also work with Government organisations, sports governing bodies, charities and the NHS.

There are many ways for SMEs to benefit from the wealth of knowledge and expertise at Loughborough University – some of them partially funded.

Access is easy. Our business development team can connect you to the most relevant expertise in a number of ways including industrial collaborations, technology licensing, bespoke training, Continuing Professional Development and consultancy services.

We specialise in assembling interdisciplinary teams of experts from across the University to tackle real-world problems and issues. Our six interdisciplinary Research Challenges facilitate work across traditional academic boundaries:

Changing environments and Infrastructure
Tackling the challenges to global economies and ecosystems presented by climate, land use and hydrological change.

Communication, Culture and Citizenship
Understanding the processes which trigger inclusion and exclusion – contributing to more equal and just societies.

Enabling Technologies
Developing cutting-edge manufacturing solutions, technologies and materials innovations whilst accelerating pathways to impact to realise economic and societal benefit.

Energy
Reducing energy demand; increasing energy efficiency; and developing affordable, low-carbon technologies to create a decarbonised-energy future.

Health and Wellbeing
Applying our expertise in sports science, design, manufacturing and engineering to accelerate regenerative medicine and lifestyle interventions.

Secure and Resilient Societies
Developing risk reduction and rapid emergency response strategies, and creating cutting-edge security technologies.

AN EXCELLENT BASE FOR YOUR BUSINESS
Occupying 63,000m^2 floor space, Loughborough University Science and Enterprise Parks is one of the largest Science Parks in the UK. As well as fully-serviced office and laboratory space at the heart of our thriving innovation community, businesses also benefit from access to research expertise, undergraduate and research students for projects and placements, and graduates for employment.

01509 223110 | enterprise@lboro.ac.uk | www.lboro.ac.uk/enterprise

CASE STUDIES – LOUGHBOROUGH UNIVERSITY

Apical – beyond 3D and HD

A TSB-funded Knowledge Transfer Partnership between Loughborough University's Department of Computer Science and advanced image processing technology company Apical is pushing back the boundaries of cutting-edge imaging systems.

The Loughborough research team worked with Apical to develop an end-to-end HDR video capture, delivery and display system suitable for viewing across a range of devices including Android and iPhone handsets, laptops and PCs, and HD and 3D televisions.

Based on current SDR video coding techniques and Apical's market leading display enhancement technology – IridixTM – the team has developed a system that is adaptive to extreme viewing conditions, fully backward-compatible, saves energy and is suitable for the full range of display devices serving the mobile, broadband and broadcast sectors.

Impact

- The team has developed and tested the system with the cooperation of two of Apical's clients – both world-leaders in the mobile and broadband sectors
- A commercial prototype system for digital TV broadcast has been developed and is awaiting commercial testing

Intelligent Energy

Intelligent Energy – the global power technology company – is founded on Loughborough research and continues to enjoy close ties with the University.

Headquartered on Loughborough University Science and Enterprise Parks, Intelligent Energy works with Loughborough experts and partners bluechip companies, OEMs and public research programmes to accelerate the global deployment of clean technology for the automotive, consumer electronics, and distributed power and generation markets.

IP-rich – with over 25 years in R&D – the company holds over 550 patents (granted/pending) and employs more than 350 people, many of whom are Loughborough graduates.

In July 2014, the company successfully launched on the London Stock Exchange – at a rate sufficient to qualify for inclusion in the FTSE 250 index.

Impact and key milestones

- 2008 – the world's first fuel cell powered manned flight
- 2012 – spearheaded a consortium to bring fuel cell electric black taxis to London
- 2014 – launched Upp™, a personal energy device
    - provided cost-efficient clean power for India's telecom towers
    - launched on the London Stock Exchange

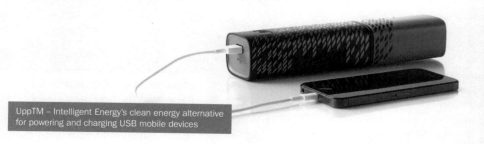

UppTM – Intelligent Energy's clean energy alternative for powering and charging USB mobile devices

University knowledge, powering business innovation

Manchester Metropolitan University

At MMU, we recognise the important role that universities have to play in wider society and we are committed to ensuring that all new knowledge generated at MMU has economic, social, cultural and environmental benefits.

Whether you're looking for strategic business or marketing support, product and service design, or a fresh perspective on the challenges you face, we are here to provide creative solutions through our training and CPD, contract and collaborative research, knowledge transfer partnerships and specialist facility hire. MMU has an impressive track-record of harnessing its expertise to help drive forward businesses, public sector and other organisations. You'll see evidence of this in our case studies.

How does it work?

Consultancy and contract research is where our academic experts become your expert consultants. An established and successful way to inject new knowledge into your organisation.

Our award winning Knowledge Transfer Partnerships (KTP) projects are a highly cost effective way to access academic consultants whilst utilising our brightest students. A KTP places a jointly selected high quality graduate, supported by a leading academic expert for between 6 months and 3 years, to work on a specific project that will significantly and permanently improve your business performance. Projects focus on innovative solutions to generate new products, develop markets, improve operating processes and systems or increase sustainability.

Bespoke Training and CPD can enhance and improve individual performance in the workplace for the long term. Courses are bespoke specific to business needs.

Our specialist facilities and laboratories are equipped with the latest research instrumentation and are maintained to the highest standards and have the added benefit of experienced professional and technical expertise to hand.

"University knowledge and research is about transforming lives and goes at the heart of what a University is about. We achieve this not just through our own wonderful and engaged staffing and student base, but also, and more importantly, the people that we work hand-in-hand with to effect a positive change in the economy and society. We work alongside business and industrial partners, local and national Government and policymakers, public sector organisations, community groups, charities and NGOs, schools, colleges and of course the wider public in Manchester and beyond. We are a 'situated' university. The impact of our work is felt and recognised on a national and international scale, but this is only possible because of the fantastic heritage and innovation of the city and region in which we serve."

Professor Jean–Noël Ezingeard
Deputy Vice-Chancellor for Research and Strategic Planning

Manchester Metropolitan University
Expertise for business, public sector & communities

Call: 0161 247 2186
Email: conversation@mmu.ac.uk
Visit: www.mmu.ac.uk/business

University knowledge, powering business innovation

Manchester Metropolitan University

The Client

The Village Bakery Ltd. Small to medium-sized enterprise (SME) based in Wrexham, Wales. Family-owned bakery producing wide range of savoury pastries and 'morning goods' via shops, wholesale business and national retailers.

The Project

The client recognised that to maintain competitive edge within the dynamic food market, it had to keep evolving. They needed to develop a new range of gluten-free products, so approached Manchester Metropolitan University about a knowledge transfer partnership (KTP) because of its expertise in food technology.

The Results

Facilitated move into a profitable niche market, achieving sales of £6m, £2m NPT, 52% market share and exports of £360k (within 2 years).
Established new accredited bakery, with 46 skilled jobs created.
Waste levels decreased (16% to 0.07%) and customer complaints were reduced by 80%.
Access to university facilities and expertise to develop products.
Developed technical skills and expertise, e.g. functionality of food ingredients.
Raised company profile and enhanced reputation, enabling further business developments with major retailers.

The Client

Wulvern Housing is the largest housing association in South Cheshire, providing homes and services for over 11,000 customers. Housing Associations are non-profit and provide affordable homes for people in need.

The Project

The core aim of the project was to reduce void properties and rent losses and to improve the quality of the housing stock, through rigorous monitoring and evaluation. MMU Cheshire worked closely with Wulvern Housing to address key strategic and developmental areas within the housing sector.

The Results

- Developed the WINS tool, Wulvern Indicators of Neighbourhood Sustainability. A sophisticated diagnostic sustainability tool used to:
  - Enhance core operations
  - Focus actions and investments in construction
  - Repair and modernise to improve demand
  - Improve customer satisfaction and neighbourhood improvement.
- Improved data capture and analysis, steering future investments in planning, housing developments and maintenance, and further supporting neighbourhood regeneration and wider green issues for future investments.

Nottingham Trent University

Working with a university is a cost-effective way to access the latest thinking and technology. Nottingham Trent University (NTU) academic staff sit at the forefront of industry developments and knowledge. This makes their understanding and experience invaluable to organisations nationally and internationally. We work with businesses of all sizes, in all sectors, helping them to commercialise their ideas and develop new and improved products and services by providing access to University knowledge, expertise and facilities.

Capturing grants to help you innovate

Our Grant Capture Team help transform original ideas into commercial opportunities. If you have a technology-based project which can demonstrate the potential for a high level of innovation, impact and challenge, then there is a potential funding opportunity waiting for you. The team provides expert advice and support for partnerships applying for funding, from organisations such as the European Union, the Technology Strategy Board (TSB), charities and trusts.

We also offer Knowledge Transfer Partnerships (KTPs). These projects are designed to provide solutions for a strategic business need, where a graduate works within a company, while being supported by University experts. Projects typically involve the development of new products, processes and systems. Funding of 50% – 67% of the cost is available, depending on the size of company and length of project.

Working with you...

Small and medium businesses have a huge impact on the UK economy, and NTU are committed to helping them develop their full potential. We have made significant investment in programmes aimed at supporting small and medium businesses in the East Midlands. Part funded by the European Regional Development Fund (ERDF), these programmes offer subsidised, and in some cases free, support to eligible organisations.

Talent, skills and innovation

Whether you are a small business or multi-national corporation we can tailor our support to fit your needs. We offer a variety of business services, including;

- Talent: Whether you are interested in graduate recruitment, student placements, or some help to solve a specific problem, our students and graduates can add real value to your business.

- Skills: From short courses to postgraduate degrees, our learning and development programmes can be tailored to help your career, or develop your workforce.

- Innovation: Many of our experts have industry experience and our real-world research and consultancy can bring about practical change and improvements to any business.

Whatever the business need, we will work with you to get to the heart of the challenge.

Contact our dedicated business-facing team who will discuss your requirements and work with you to identify solutions.

NTU Business Development Team

Tel: +44 (0)115 848 8899
Email: workingwithyou@ntu.ac.uk
Visit **www.ntu.ac.uk/business** to find out more.

Case study

Knowledge Transfer Partnership – exploring renewable heat generation

Alkane Energy is the UK's leading coal mine methane producer and one of the UK's fastest growing independent power generators. Utilising gas from abandoned coal mines to generate green energy, Alkane's clean technology power plants contribute significantly to the UK's efforts to reduce the emission of harmful CO_2 emissions. Alkane approached Nottingham Trent University for assistance with research and practical development of a new viable revenue stream.

Challenge:

Alkane operates in a number of former coal mining areas that have been impacted by flooding. This cuts off gas flow paths, rendering the sites redundant in terms of gas extraction and electricity generation. However the depth, volume and the even temperature of the water bodies within the mines represents a vast latent heat resource.

Alkane approached NTU for assistance with research and practical development of a scheme to utilise ground source heat pumps and water in these abandoned mines.

Solution:

The company received free initial support from NTU, part-funded by the European Regional Development Fund (ERDF). This included academic research, design and development of a pump, and energy and cost analysis of the project to ensure economic viability. This has led to a two year Knowledge Transfer Partnership (KTP) project funded by the Technology Strategy Board (TSB).

The KTP is closely aligned to some of the existing core academic areas in which NTU specialises. The University is providing academic and technical support to help the company successfully harness this huge potential. The project utilises a past, and otherwise redundant, industrial legacy – the abandoned mines. It aims to develop the UK's first large scale commercial mine water-sourced heat.

Benefits:

The KTP with Alkane is still on-going but has already delivered significant benefits including:

- carbon emissions reduced by 75%;
- operating costs reduced by 50%;
- interest from several local authorities to use the system to heat their buildings; and
- confirmation of further EU funding to develop the infrastructure in other locations.

Contact us to find out how your organisation could benefit from a Knowledge Transfer Partnership.

NTU Business Development Team
Tel: +44 (0)115 848 8899
Email: workingwithyou@ntu.ac.uk

Visit **www.ntu.ac.uk/business** to find out more.

Profile

University of Surrey

The University of Surrey is internationally recognised for its innovative approach to Enterprise. Fundamental to our identity is the desire to both create new understanding and to pass it on. We conduct industry relevant research focussing on areas of strength which have impact. Ninety-nine percent of our research units were rated world-leading or internationally excellent, or were recognised internationally or nationally in the latest government review of outputs.

Our research brings benefits to many sectors, helping industry maintain its competitive edge through collaboration with us and access to our expertise, and as a top 10 university our portfolio is wide-ranging. We have many centres of excellence where we collaborate and partner with industry. For example;

- **The Centre for Communications Systems Research (CCSR),** one of the largest mobile communications groups in Europe (with a top research rating), focussing on the Internet of Things, intelligent transportation, 'smart cities', Future Internet technologies, and the Connected Digital Economy. The CCSR is also home to the development of the **world's first 5G Innovation Centre**

- **The Surrey Space Centre (SSC)**, one of the largest university satellite engineering groups globally with expertise that includes spacecraft engineering, data assimilation, radar and optical remote sensing and applications and technologies for atmospheric monitoring

- **Our new Veterinary School**, opening soon, a Centre of Excellence embracing the '**One Health – One Medicine**' philosophy, to pioneer and foster interdisciplinary collaborations in health care for humans and animals, and

- **The Surrey Business School**, emphasising the need for business research and teaching to be aligned with the fast changing nature of the economy. Through springboards like 'Agile Innovation' the School builds substantive bridges to science and technology interests, helping to accelerate the commercialisation of innovation. The development of flagship initiatives such as its **Business Insights Lab** signals its commitment to becoming a pro-active catalyst for economic growth, including the SME community.

Here at Surrey we are also home to one of the largest Electronic Engineering research groups in the UK (with a top research rating), and one of the largest Vision, Speech and Signal Processing research groups in the UK (also with a top research rating)

Our **Surrey Business Incubator in partnership with SETsquared, is ranked 1st in Europe and 2nd in the world** by the Universities Business Incubator (UBI) Index. **Our technology and space incubators** located in the **Surrey Technology Centre** support the University's incubation and acceleration strategy. Located on the University's world class **Surrey Research Park** we have a successful and long established track record in supporting and nurturing start-up activity, underpinned by our own angel investment network - the Surrey 100 Club.

In summary, there are many ways in which we work with business. Through programmes such as Knowledge Transfer Partnerships, Consultancy and Expert services, bespoke Continuous Professional Development (CPD), Collaborative and Contract Research, and Technology Transfer **we link our academic expertise with the business challenges of today and tomorrow.** Our **friendly Research and Enterprise Support team** based in the heart of the campus is here to connect you to the right place and the right person anywhere in the University today.

To find out more contact: businessdevelopment@surrey.ac.uk

Case study

Material characterisation: Knowledge Transfer Partnerships (KTPs)

The facilities at the University of Surrey are well-equipped for the micro- and nano-characterisation of bulk and thin film materials. In collaboration with Industrial Partners, PlasmaQuest Ltd and Torr Scientific Ltd, academics at the University have demonstrated their expertise in these characterisation techniques to further the development of thin film materials and XPS instrumentation.

PlasmaQuest Ltd (PQL) specialised in the deposition of thin films for functional, mechanical or corrosion resistance applications. PQL collaborated with the University of Surrey to develop materials characterisation procedures using sophisticated equipment at the University, enabling the company to significantly improve its patented deposition processes and develop new products. To fully optimise the process parameters and demonstrate thin film quality, sophisticated high capital cost analytical techniques were required. Dr Mark Baker, Reader in Surface Science and Engineering, and the KTP Associate, Hayley Brown, established protocols for each of the analytical techniques so that a rapid and reliable analysis could be undertaken on the thin films. The resultant information has enabled PQL to develop a more fundamental understanding of their patented deposition process, rapidly optimise the production process for new high-quality thin films and enhance its marketing information.

Torr Scientific Limited (TSL) specialises in the manufacture and supply of x-ray and vacuum components used in XPS systems. TSL collaborated with the University of Surrey to develop a novel x-ray monochromator based on Torr Scientific's leading-edge diamond anode technology. Surrey offered expertise in coating architectures required to produce durable thin films employed in the monochromator, valuable knowledge of the XPS user community, and test facilities using one of its two XPS spectrometers. David Bates, Managing Director at TSL commented: "We are delighted to work with the University of Surrey on this project. The expertise and facilities offered by the University is invaluable for the company's development and future growth plans."

Benefits and impact

For PQL, the KTP project has resulted in increased revenue and has enabled the company to become a leader in its field. The skills base of PQL's research scientists and engineers has been significantly enhanced.

For TSL, the ability to design and produce a high specification monochromator for surface science instrumentation introduces an important expansion of their product range. The project made a key contribution to the technological development and user insight required to bring an optimum monochromator product to market.

Sharing knowledge to help business is A-rated at

TEESSIDE UNIVERSITY

Left to right are Nahim Iqbal, Peter Barker and Professor Nashwan Dawood

An innovative Teesside University business partnership has been rated as outstanding – achieving another grade A ranking from the Technology Strategy Board.

It means that 71% of the University's recent Knowledge Transfer Partnerships (KTPs) have now been awarded grade A – the highest grade possible – compared with just 8% nationally.

KTPs see talented graduates working in a business to help improve competitiveness and productivity through better use of knowledge, technology and skills. Businesses also get the benefit of specialist support from University experts.

The latest grade A accolade is for a partnership with national company Ryder Architecture – and it's the fifth grade A for KTPs in the University's School of Science & Engineering.

Nahim Iqbal, who graduated from Teesside University with an MSc in Project Management in 2011, was employed as an associate to work with Ryder Architecture, under the supervision of Professor Nashwan Dawood.

The two-year project developed Building Information Modelling (BIM) systems to integrate into Ryder's own project design and management systems, and was such a success that Nahim has now been taken on as a full-time member of staff as BIM Development Leader.

Nahim said: 'The partnership played an integral role in advancing my skills and knowledge in the domain of design and construction. The focus on integrated research and practical experience provided a unique opportunity to engage with the wider industry and support collaboration and innovation.'

Professor Dawood added: 'The collaboration with Ryder provided a way for the company to develop new environmental, cost and construction design methodologies which will help them develop and expand their capabilities and improve business opportunities.'

Laura Woods, the University's Director of Academic Enterprise, added: 'A KTP is ideal for a company needing expert help with a specific project, perhaps to introduce new technology or new working practices. As well as a full-time graduate on the staff, the company gets academic support to deliver its improvement programme. This is just one of the direct ways that businesses can benefit from a partnership with the University.'

Be inspired – contact us now

T: 01642 384068
E: business@tees.ac.uk
tees.ac.uk/business

TEESSIDE UNIVERSITY

£12m Phoenix Building – home to DigitalCity

esside University is
namic, energetic and
novative – providing
portunities, driving
terprise and delivering
cellence. It is founded
a rich past with over
years' experience of
novation in education
nce its foundation as
nstantine College in 1930.

esside is the proud recipient of
e Queen's Anniversary Prize for
gher and Further Education 2013,
arded for outstanding work in
e field of enterprise and business
gagement, and is accredited with
e Customer First standard for its
rvices to business. It is the first

modern university in the UK to be
named the *Times Higher Education's*
University of the Year – securing
the Best Employer Engagement
award in the same year, and has
twice been shortlisted as the UK's
Entrepreneurial University of the
Year.

With a growing reputation as a
leading business-facing University,
Teesside has been described by
Dr Vince Cable, Secretary of State
for Business, Innovation and Skills
as 'Britain's best university for
working with business'.

Teesside is renowned for its
commitment to enterprise and
entrepreneurship with a legacy

of successful spin-out companies,
helping to create 240 companies
and over 400 jobs through its
work with business. It has leading
expertise in applied STEM and
health disciplines, and specifically
in digital, crime and society, the
arts, and design, and is home to
DigitalCity – with Middlesbrough a
national hub for the development
of digital enterprise in the fields of
animation, gaming and web.

The University's successful
relationships with business deliver
lasting benefits to the economy
through initiatives such as
high-quality knowledge transfer
partnerships (KTPs) and sector-
leading workforce development
provision. It also provides a
range of specialist business
services, including student and
graduate placements, advice and
guidance for new companies,
specialist technical facilities and
accommodation for conferences
and meetings.

THE QUEEN'S
ANNIVERSARY PRIZES
FOR HIGHER AND FURTHER EDUCATION
2013

Be inspired – contact us now

T: 01642 384068
E: business@tees.ac.uk
tees.ac.uk/business

Index of Advertisers